THE STORY
OF GOLF

THE STORY
OF GOLF

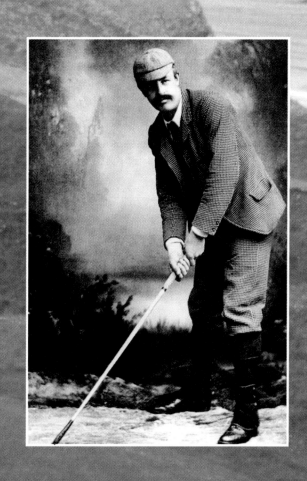

GEORGE PEPER

Foreword by Jack Nicklaus

The author wishes to thank his colleague
and friend Jim Frank for the many contribu-
tions he made to the final text, including
major additions to several chapters.
Thanks also go to Dana Belina for her
help in researching and collecting the
historical photos that illustrate the book.

Publisher's Cataloging-in-Publication
Peper, George.
    The story of golf / George Peper; foreword
by Jack Nicklaus. — 1st ed.
     p. cm.
    Includes bibliographical references and index.
     ISBN: 1-57500-039-3
     1.Golf—History. I. Title.
  GV968.P47 1999   796.352
            QB199-133

The Story of Golf is the companion book to the documentary on public television.

Book design by Tania Garcia

Credits for illustrations will be found on p. 224.

The publisher has made every effort to secure permission to reproduce copyrighted material and would like to apologize should there have been any errors or omissions.

TV Books, L.L.C.
Publishers serving the television industry.
1619 Broadway, Ninth Floor, New York, NY 10019
www.tvbooks.com

Title page: Tralee Golf Club, Tralee, Ireland.
Title page inset: English essayist Horace Hutchinson at St. Andrews.

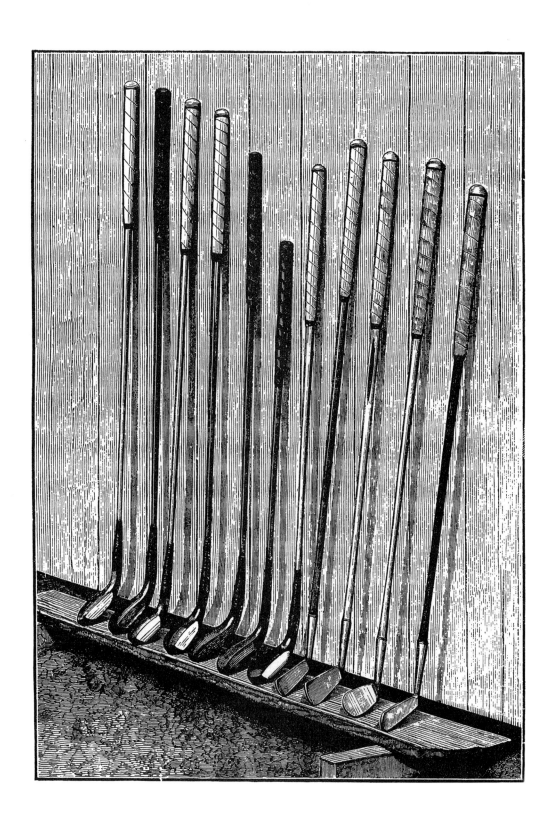

Contents

FOREWORD

Jack Nicklaus

I have always been interested in the traditions and history of the game of golf. What true disciple of the game would not be curious to explore its origins some six hundred years ago and to trace its evolution into the game we play and love today?

From initiation to completion late in 1998, "The Story of Golf" was a ten-year project. Over that period its producers consulted almost every major historical authority, both individuals and organizations, in the United Kingdom, golf's birthplace, as well as in the United States, where the game has grown prolifically. They tackled an immense and complex subject, with incomparable results.

Particularly responsible for the program's historical breadth, accuracy, and integrity was principal researcher and scriptwriter George Peper, Editor in Chief of GOLF Magazine, one of the world's foremost golf periodicals. The creative team also received considerable help and encouragement from the game's two leading governing bodies, the Royal and Ancient Golf Club of St. Andrews and the United States Golf Association.

So excited were its principals as they recorded "The Story of Golf" that they decided to offer the film to the home-video market and develop the project into book form. Although I am no historian, I cannot imagine that a more comprehensive, entertaining, and faithful chronicle of this greatest game exists beyond their two-hour program or the following pages.

Ardent golfers and avid history buffs will enjoy this wonderfully informative and fascinating book. I am sure it will be a favorite addition to your library.

CHAPTER I

Stick and Ball Games

Where it began, no one knows. The origin is lost in the mists of time.

It might have been on a country road in Normandy, or in an alley near the Roman forum. It might have been among sand dunes above the North Sea, or on a hillside overlooking Peking. It might have been in a field in Flanders or a courtyard in London or on the frozen surface of a Dutch canal.

No one can say precisely where or when the game of golf was born, but one thing is certain: No other form of recreation has transfixed its practitioners with such engaging appeal.

Today, as we approach the twenty-first century, hardly a country in the civilized world remains untouched by the glorious epidemic that is golf. Its lure is difficult to define and impossible to exaggerate — an obsession that can begin at any age and last a lifetime.

The elemental appeal of golf stems from one of man's primal instincts: the urge to strike an object with a stick. Indeed, reasonable skill in club-swinging surely was key to the survival of the caveman. It's not hard to envision *homo erectus* hefting a sturdy tree limb to swat at stones or bones or whatever came into his path. In this sense, the notion — or at least the motion — of golf is older than civilization itself. Fundamentally, golf was not invented but was born within us.

But it was civilization that gave the game its spin. Depending on whom we choose to believe, the first primeval golf shots were struck somewhere between two thousand and six hundred years ago. The earliest possible ancestor dates to the Roman Empire. It seems that the Roman soldiers were enthusiastic sportsmen, and one of the ways they kept in fighting trim was by playing *paganica,* a game in which they swatted at a feather-stuffed ball with curved sticks. But all evidence suggests that this was a team sport, and that the ball the troops were striking was moving, not stationary. Thus, if *paganica* was the forerunner of a modern game, it was more likely field hockey than golf.

Illustrated scrolls from the early Ming Dynasty (mid- to late-1300s) depict something called *suigan,* described as "a game in which you hit a ball with a stick while walking." At least one scholar has suggested that the silk traders of the late Middle Ages might have exported this or a similar game to Europe, where it was spun and refined into golf.

A stained glass window in England's Gloucester Cathedral, dating from the mid-fourteenth century, shows a figure wielding a stick in the middle of a distinctly golf-like backswing. Was this golf? Possibly. But it might also have been another stick-and-ball game, with the exotic name *cambuca,* which was known to be played in England at the time.

Across the English Channel, the French had taken to a rather genteel courtyard game called *jeu de mail.* Originally developed in Italy, it was a curious blend of billiards, croquet, and miniature golf, played with long-handled mallets and large wooden balls within a well-defined area. The object was to hit the ball through one or more iron hoops, using the fewest possible strokes.

Opposite above: Scrolls from the Ming Dynasty suggest the Chinese may have been the first golfers.

Opposite below: A golf-like swing, circa 1350, from a window of the Gloucester Cathedral.

Chapter opener: Mary, Queen of Scots, playing golf at St. Andrews, 1563.

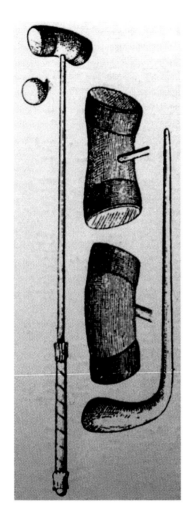

Above: The implements of *jeu de mail,* a mixture of billiards, croquet and golf.

Opposite: In the eighteenth century the Basques played a cross-country version of *jeu de mail.*

Jeu de mail caught on briefly in England where it became the rage of the ruling class under the name "pall mall." It was first played in London on the street with the same name, which now runs between Buckingham Palace and Piccadilly Circus. Back in 1629, King Charles I was an avid pall maller, and the court of St. James included an impressive one thousand-yard-long area for royal play.

By the eighteenth century, however, this game had played out except in southern France, where a more expansive version saw the Basques hitting over hill and dale to targets such as the sides of barns and pasture gates. Shades of golf there, for sure.

Meanwhile, in Belgium they were hooked on *chole,* a game with a delightfully spiteful quality. It was played cross country, usually in teams, with the players wielding heavy iron clubs to propel an egg-shaped wooden ball distances of up to four hundred yards. A target — a church door, a tree, almost anything — was established, sometimes as much as a mile away, and then the two teams bid on the number of shots needed to hit it. The low-bidding team led off by taking three strokes toward the target. Then the opponents — known as *decholeurs* — were allowed one stroke to send the ball into the nastiest possible trouble. Thereafter, the offense resumed pursuit with three more strokes, followed by one more for the defense, and so on until the bid was either hit or missed.

But whether these games of the Renaissance era bore any resemblance to golf is of little consequence, because by that time golf itself was well entrenched along the eastern coast of Scotland.

Indeed, the best candidate for a true forefather of the Scottish game comes from the people across the North Sea, the Dutch, who back in the thirteenth century were playing a game that bears a more than passing similarity to golf. And the name of that game? Colf, spelled *c-o-l-f.*

As early as 1296 the Dutch had a *colf* course, and a formidable one at that. It stretched forty-five hundred yards for just four holes — except that they weren't holes, they were doors — to a kitchen, a windmill, a castle, and a courthouse. Four-door models such as this were undoubtedly typical, but no target was off limits to the *colf*-crazed Dutchmen, who pursued their balls through churchyards, cemeteries, and smack through the centers of their own towns, often wreaking havoc with the local citizenry. The winners usually collected a barrel

Above: Evidence shows that a game called *colf* was played in Holland as early as 1296.

of beer from the losing side, which means the original "Nineteenth Hole" actually was the fifth.

Ultimately, when the toll of personal injuries and broken glass became insupportable, the "colfers" were banished to the countryside during the warmer months, and, in winter, to the frozen lakes and rivers where they directed their shots toward poles in the ice.

Numerous richly detailed landscape paintings done by the Dutch Masters show us that *colf* remained popular in Holland for at least four hundred years. By the early 1700s, however, the game had mysteriously vanished.

Where did it go? In all probability, to Scotland. After all, it doesn't take a Ph.D. in linguistics to make a connection between the words "colf" and "golf." The implements used were very similar, the balls nearly identical. And, above all, there is the compelling evidence of geography.

By 1650, golf — spelled the way we spell it today — was well-rooted in the fabric of a dozen or so cities along Scotland's east coast. One look

at the map shows that the coast was but a short sail from more than forty commercial centers of Holland. Trade between the two countries was brisk, dating back to medieval times, and evidence exists that the Scots exported wooden colf clubs to the Dutch (along with wool and other products), while the Dutch returned with rudimentary colf balls. And there are numerous paintings of the period showing Scotsmen in kilts playing a ball-and-stick game on the ice as the Dutch did.

But, no matter where the seeds of golf were sown, without question it was the Scots who gave the game its unique character, the Scots who combined the elements of distance off the tee and deftness into the green, and the Scots who ingrained the notion of each player advancing independently toward the hole, without interference from his opponents. (The Scots were largely Calvinists, who knew that the greatest sins, deserving the greatest punishment, always came from within. How perfectly applicable to golf.)

From the very beginning, this game was dangerously addictive. Indeed, the first written evidence of golf is a parliamentary decree

Above: Colf was a recurrent subject in the landscapes of The Dutch Masters.

Overleaf: Most golf historians agree that the game as we know it came from the Scots.

Above: The marriage of Scotland's James IV to an English princess was good news for golfers.

banning it for reasons of national security. In 1457, King James II of Scotland declared "that futeball and golfe be utterly cryit doune and nocht usit." Back then, the Scots were at war with England and the principal weapons of combat were the bow and arrow. But it seems the Scottish lads had been neglecting their archery practice in favor of golf.

Similar edicts were issued in the subsequent reigns of James III and IV... and were largely ignored. But when James IV married the daughter of England's King Henry IV, the conflict with the English suddenly ended — and so did the conflict with golfers. In fact, James IV himself became the first of a long line of royals who took to the links. In the account books of his court it is noted that funds were spent for the purchase of golf clubs and balls, and there also is the settling of a golf bet which the king lost. Legend also holds that in 1567 Mary Queen of Scots was so smitten with the game that she teed up the day after her husband, Lord Darnley, was murdered; this was, in fact, one of the charges leveled against her that eventually cost her the crown, her head, and a chance to win the rubber match.

In 1604, the King of England appointed a royal clubmaker, and soon after that, a seven-hole course was laid out near London on the Black Heath by the River Thames. Nearly four hundred years later, Royal Blackheath still sits there, although it wasn't established as a club until 1766.

Despite the royal seal of approval, golf in those days was an equal opportunity pastime, open to anyone with a couple of clubs, a ball, and the urge for some light exercise. One of the first written accounts of the game — a description of play on the Links of Leith, near Edinburgh — extols its democratic spirit.

"The greatest and wisest of the land were to be seen mingling freely with the humblest mechanics in the pursuit of their common and beloved amusement. All distinctions of rank were leveled by the joyous spirit of the game."

It was an informal, almost free-form activity back then, with no rules, few guidelines (although playing on the Sabbath was, for a time, illegal), and no tournaments or competitions except for casual matches among friends. All evidence suggests that the Scots played this disorganized brand of golf for at least three centuries.

Just as disorganized, certainly by modern standards, were the

methods used to play the early game. Instead of one way to swing there were as many swings as there were villages with courses of their own. The townspeople tended to copy the technique of the local champion, who usually hit on a set-up and swing that allowed him to conquer the vagaries of his local weather.

The Scottish coast is constantly buffeted by sea breezes, so the most successful golfers learned to hit the ball on a low trajectory that kept it under the wind. To accomplish this, they learned to spread their feet far apart (as much as a yard), aim their bodies to the right of the target, position the ball well back in the stance, and bend their knees deeply. Then they whipped the club around their bodies (rather than up and down, as we do today) on a markedly horizontal plane that further encouraged low flight. The ball flew just a few feet off the ground, traveling only about 150 yards, and would then run a long way after hitting the hard turf of the windblown links.

As the game spread, more methods and champions developed. Word of great play traveled from town to town. And, inevitably, a desire arose to determine the best golfer in the land. It was at that point that the game as we know it began to take shape.

Above: An early competition at Royal Blackheath, the first golf club in England.

CHAPTER 2

Made in Scotland

In March 1744, a group of golfers who played over the Links at Leith persuaded the city of Edinburgh to provide a silver club as the prize for an annual competition. The event was open to "as many Noblemen or Gentlemen or other Golfers, from any part of Great Britain or Ireland" as would send in their entries. The winner was to be called "The Captain of the Golf," and would become the arbiter of all disputes touching the game.

The response was a bit underwhelming. Only a dozen men signed up—all of them local lads—and only ten played, with the prize going to an Edinburgh surgeon named John Rattray with a score of 60 for two trips around the five-hole course. That wasn't too bad considering the holes ranged from 414 to 495 yards, which one golf historian estimates would equal holes of six hundred yards today, given our modern equipment. Nonetheless, this modest event is generally recognized as golf's first organized competition, and the Leith golfers are credited with forming the game's first bona fide club, the Honourable Company of Edinburgh Golfers. Over the next few generations, this group would move numerous times, always keeping their name intact, eventually settling to the east of Edinburgh at Muirfield, their current home, in 1891.

Below: The original thirteen Rules of Golf, published in 1744.

Opposite: The linksland of St. Andrews has been in play for eight centuries, perhaps more.

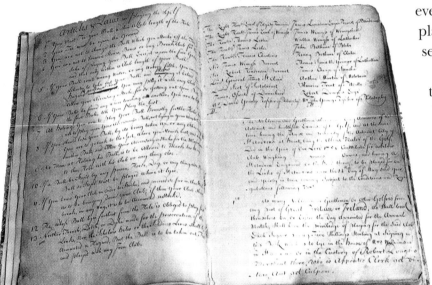

Ah, but on that day in 1744 something even more important happened: Golf was played for the first time according to a set of rules.

They were admirably brief—just thirteen edicts in all (today's Rule book is 120 pages long!)—and admirably charitable as well, with no penalties for violations. This set of simple, straightforward principles would prevail virtually unchanged for nearly a century.

Among the provisos: "If your ball is stopped by any person, horse, dog, or anything else, the ball must be played as it lies," and "If your club snaps and breaks in the course of the downswing, you are deemed to have made a stroke." And perhaps most illuminating, the first rule: "You must tee your ball within a club-length of the hole." Imagine how frustratingly craggy those early putting greens must have been!

Indeed, golf's first playing fields bore little resemblance to the manicured meadows we enjoy today. The handful of courses that dotted the coast of Scotland were set on linksland, the barren, undulating, windswept terrain that separated the beach from the arable ground further inland. During the Ice Age the sea had covered these

areas so the subsoil was sandy, which meant it drained well but supported only long grasses and thick brush, making it of little value except as a home to rabbits and sheep.

In fact, it was these hungry herbivores who served as golf's first and most stalwart greenskeepers. Bear in mind that the game was played for about four hundred years before any human got around to cutting the grass.

The animals also took a leading role in golf course design by burrowing their way into the turf as protection against the elements. When, over time, the wind enlarged those burrows, golf's oldest and meanest hazard — the bunker — took shape.

Yes, those original courses were less fashioned by man than formed by nature. There were no tees, no fairways, and no greens as such, just a hole in the ground every few hundred yards. And even those holes were a bit unpredictable. One might be as shallow as a rabbit scrape, the next so deep that simply retrieving one's ball was a major assignment.

There was no set number of holes for a round of golf, either. From town to town, variety was the name of the game as each course ran according to the flow of the land. A round thus consisted of one or more turns around whatever number of holes the locals happened to favor. While the Links at Leith was five holes, nearby North Berwick sported seven. Meanwhile, there was a twelve-holer at Prestwick, on Scotland's west coast, and Montrose, on the North Sea, weighed in with a whopping twenty-five.

In time, of course, a standard would be set. And the authority for that decree, as well as countless later rulings on the game, would come from the abiding bastion of golf administration, the town of St. Andrews.

Set on a remote bulge of Scotland's east coast, this unassuming little town would seem a most unlikely seat of authority of any kind. Yet St. Andrews has been the ecclesiastical heart of Scotland since the twelfth century, a religious Mecca equal to Canterbury in England. It is also the home of the oldest university in Scotland.

And, for generations of golfers, St. Andrews has meant one thing: the grandest of all links, the Old Course, a magnificent stretch of rolling terrain set hard by a bay of the North Sea. Written evidence of golf at St. Andrews dates from 1552, but most historians agree that the game was

Opposite: Golf's first greenskeepers were grazing, burrowing sheep.

Above: As wind enlarged the burrows, bunkers were born.

Overleaf: Golf's cradle, the "Old Grey Toun" of St. Andrews.

played there in one form or another for at least three hundred years before that, perhaps by shepherds swinging crooks as the first cleeks.

In 1890, Horace Hutchinson, an English essayist and inveterate St. Andrews golfer, captured the cachet of the "Old Grey Toun" with words that ring equally true today: "When two stranger golfers meet upon some neutral ground, one of the first questions that will pass from one to the other will most certainly be 'Have you been to St. Andrews?' and should the answer be in the negative the questioner will immediately deem himself justified in assuming a tone of patronage which the other will feel he has no right to resent."

The golfers of St. Andrews did not organize themselves into a club until 1754, ten years after the men of Leith. On May 14, "twenty-two Noblemen and Gentlemen being admirers of the ancient and healthfull exercise of the Golf" formed The Society of St. Andrews Golfers. They immediately adopted the thirteen rules set down by the golfers of Edinburgh. They also adopted the Honourable Company's habit of dressing for play in bright red coats, the better to be seen by the locals who used the same linksland for strolling, doing the laundry, and picnicking. But despite following Edinburgh's lead, it was almost inevitable that this small town would assume an administrative role equal to the stature it had already earned as the golf capital of the world.

The first step in that direction came in 1764, when the St. Andreans made a drastic revision to their hallowed playground. At that time, the Old Course consisted of twelve holes, set on a long narrow strip along the shore. The golfers played eleven holes out to the far end of the course, then turned and threaded their way home, playing ten of the holes backward to the same cups before finishing at a solitary hole near where they'd started. Thus, a round at St. Andrews consisted of twenty-two holes.

Below: A 1798 competition among members of the Society of St. Andrews Golfers.

Opposite: English essayist Horace Hutchinson was a dedicated St. Andrews golfer.

WILLIAM·IV

But in 1764, the Society of St. Andrews Golfers decided to convert the first four holes of the course into two. This trimming may have been precipitated by a record round: Earlier that year, William St. Clair played the twenty-two holes in 121 strokes, an average of 5.5 strokes per hole. Since this change automatically shortened the same four holes to two on the road in, the St. Andrews round was reduced from twenty-two holes to eighteen, the number that would become standard throughout the world. (Due to subsequent changes, including widening the fairways and enlarging the greens, the Old Course that we know today wasn't really in play until the early 1840s.)

Over the next several years, the Society would attract the best and brightest golfers and gentlemen, frame a new set of rules, and generally position itself as the last word on all questions related to the game, even setting the standard for the size of the cups cut in the green (4¼ inches). When, in 1834, England's King William IV became the patron of the Society and declared it the Royal & Ancient Golf Club, the enduring preeminence of St. Andrews was assured.

Back in 1834, however, there wasn't much golf to oversee. Only seventeen clubs existed: fourteen in Scotland, two in England, and one in, of all places, India, at the Royal Calcutta Golf Club, where a group of British colonials had brought the game.

In all the world, at that time, fewer than a thousand people could call themselves golfers. And more than a few were women.

In 1811, the fishwives of Musselburgh participated in the first known women's-only tournament. The first club for women, the St. Andrews Ladies' Golf Club, formed in 1867 and boasted a membership of over five hundred by 1886. The Ladies' Golf Union followed in 1893, with the first official Ladies Championship not far behind. It was won, as were the two that followed, by the remarkable Lady Margaret Scott, who was known for an unusually long backswing (the club nearly hit her in the back), tremendous distance (gained, perhaps, from trying to keep up with three golfer brothers), and scores in the 80s, all while wearing the

long skirts, long sleeves, and other less-than-sporting attire expected of a woman in that era. Not much more is known about her other than that after winning her third straight championship, Lady Margaret married and retired from the game undefeated.

Doing somewhat less well, however, was the game itself. In the early 1800s golf wasn't spreading, it was shrinking. What a century earlier had been a recreation for the masses had eroded into a diversion for the wealthy and privileged. Why? Above all, because of the ball.

The very first golfers are believed to have played with balls made of boxwood, similar to the balls used in the earlier games of pall mall and *chole.* The balls were simply turned on a carpenter's lathe and, if a bit lacking in sophistication, were at least affordable.

But in the early seventeenth century a new ball was put in play. Called the feathery, it consisted of a leather cover stuffed with the breast feathers of a goose or chicken. It was about 1.6 inches in diameter (roughly the size that the ball is today), but weighed only three-quarters of an ounce, about half that of a modern ball. The feathery provided good resilience and distance: The strongest players could hit it over two hundred yards. But with this development, the making of golf balls suddenly became a fine art.

A strip of untanned bull or horse hide was soaked in alum water, then cut into three pieces—two circles and a strip for the middle. These were sewn together, soaked again, and turned inside out so the seams were on the inside. A small hole was left in this shell, and into that hole the ballmaker stuffed the feathers, which had been boiled to make them limp and malleable. He did his stuffing with the aid of a tool called a "brogue," a blunt-edged iron spike topped with a wooden crosspiece on which the ballmaker leaned with all his weight. When he had crammed in approximately a top-hat-full of feathers using the brogue, he poked in a last few with a small awl and then sewed up the hole.

Then, still wet inside and out, the ball was set out to dry. As it did, the feathers expanded while the cover contracted, thus producing a sphere of resilient hardness. The feathery was then hammered as round as possible and painted for protection against the elements.

Feathery-making was a serious business, requiring equal parts mastery and muscle, and even the best craftsmen could produce no more than four balls per day. Accordingly, featheries were extremely expensive — twelve times as costly as the old wooden balls.

What's more, for all that work, the finished product was less than a model of durability. It became waterlogged easily and one off-center slash with an iron club could literally knock the stuffing out of it. Thus, a player invariably required three or four balls per round.

Under these circumstances, only the wealthiest golfers could sustain their passion. Clearly, what was needed was a ball that would be inexpensive, weatherproof, and closer to round; a ball whose performance, durability, and affordability would attract more people to the game.

In the mid-nineteenth century, that ball arrived. It came all the way from the Far East in the form of gutta percha, the coagulated milk of a Malayan gum tree.

The precise origin of the gutta percha ball is a matter of some dispute, but surely the claim that is most exotic, if not authentic, is the saga of the Hindu Statue. It seems that James Paterson, a Scottish missionary based in India, sent a statue — actually a marble bas relief of the Hindu god Vishnu — to his brother Robert, then a ministry student in St. Andrews. The statue had been cushioned for shipment with chunks and chips of gutta percha, a moldable substance that so fascinated young Robert that he first tried to resole his boot with it. Then he fashioned it into a golf ball.

Robert Paterson played a few holes on the Old Course with his gutta percha ball in April 1845 without great consequence, then sent the ball

Opposite: By the nineteenth century women were into the game but the expensive, difficult-to-produce feathery ball made golf a game for the elite.

Below: The "gutty" restored the game to the masses.

Above: Willie Dunn, the maker of this feathery, was one of the last to convert to the gutta percha ball.

Opposite: Another late convert was the game's first great player, Allan Robertson.

to a third brother near Edinburgh, who took up the cause and began producing gutta percha balls as a business venture.

The substance was exported in the form of a sheet, which the ballmaker cut into strips, softened in hot water, and rounded into a ball by hand. The ball was then dropped into cold water to harden. It was as simple as that. (And if a gutty became a little bruised or cracked, it could be re-softened in hot water and made whole again.)

The first gutties brought mixed reaction. They were certainly rounder than the feather ball — in fact, they were nearly as smooth as billiard balls — but therein lay a problem. With no markings on their surface, they were tough to get airborne and tended to duck or dive in flight. Yet golfers didn't know that — yet.

Willie Dunn, a professional from Musselburgh, was so disgusted with the gutties' poor flight that he gave the balls to his caddies. In short time, however, he noticed that the caddies were hitting the gutty with more authority than he himself could muster from a feathery. The reason proved to be the nicks and scuffs the ball had received from iron shots: Once it had a few cuts on its face, the gutty flew like a champion. Thus, generation two became the hand-hammered gutty, with aerodynamic markings pre-chiseled onto its surface.

Here, then, was a ball that traveled farther, putted truer, and, best of all, cost far less than its feather-stuffed forerunner. In short time, entire Malayan forests were being leveled for the sake of golf as craftsmen began cranking out gutties at the rate of a hundred a day. Armed with this ball for all, thousands of tradesmen, artisans, and peasants once again joined their better-bred brethren on the links as golf was returned at last to the working man.

By 1890, the smattering of golf clubs in Great Britain would grow to 387, playing over 140 different courses. Meanwhile, outside the U.K., golf would extend its colonial tentacles to every outpost in the British Empire, reaching Australia, New Zealand, Canada, South Africa, Ceylon, Shanghai, Bangkok, and Hong Kong as well as India. A gutta percha golf boom had reignited the game.

But the arrival of the gutty was met with alarm and opposition by one faction of the golf world: the feathery makers. Chief among them was the game's first renaissance man, Allan Robertson of St. Andrews.

A sturdily-built fellow with red-brown whiskers and a perpetual smile, Allan was the last of six generations of club- and ball-making Robertsons and was also the finest golfer of his time, purportedly never losing a head-to-head match. In *Reminiscences of Golf on St. Andrews Links,* published in 1887, James Balfour described Robertson: "He was a short, little, active man, with a pleasant face, small features, and a merry twinkle in his eye. He was universally popular, not a bit forward, but withal easy and full of self-respect." Robertson is credited with being the game's first professional player (meaning he played for money) and was probably the game's first course architect and green superintendent as well, rendering an unofficial but highly valued service as tender of the St. Andrews links.

But ballmaking was Robertson's livelihood, and the gutty threatened it. At one point he became so bitter that he bought up any gutties found in the bushes of the Old Course and destroyed them by fire. Robertson also made his employees promise never to use the ball, which led to a rift between him and his chief apprentice, Tom Morris.

Six years Robertson's junior and nearly as fine a player, Morris agreed to shun the gutty, but then was caught in a transgression. He pled innocence, claiming he'd run out of featheries in mid-round and was forced to borrow a ball, but Robertson was unconvinced. The result was that Morris left his employer and opened his own shop making gutties, first in St. Andrews and later across the country in Prestwick, where he also became keeper of the green.

In time, however, even Robertson gave in to the gutty, happily finding that he could produce more balls—and income—with much less work. And, to his credit, he was among the first to realize that the new ball required a new set of clubs.

Golf had been played with essentially the same implements for more than two centuries, an assortment of idiosyncratic mallets devised to fit the rugged demands of the game. The woods, which far outnumbered the irons, had shafts made of hazelwood or ash with heads of apple or thornwood, materials hard enough to withstand impact first with wooden balls, then the alum-hardened featheries. The two pieces of wood were carefully spliced together, then glued and bound with several windings of tarred twine. The grips were soft sheepskin wrapped around the end of the shaft.

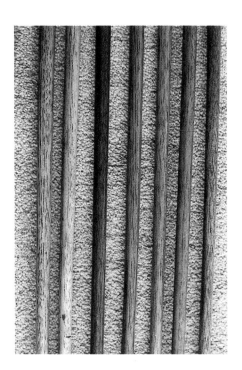

Below: With the advent of the new ball, hickory—imported from America—became the preferred wood for club shafts.

Opposite: Old Tom Morris was fired from his job as a feathery maker after he was caught playing a gutty ball.

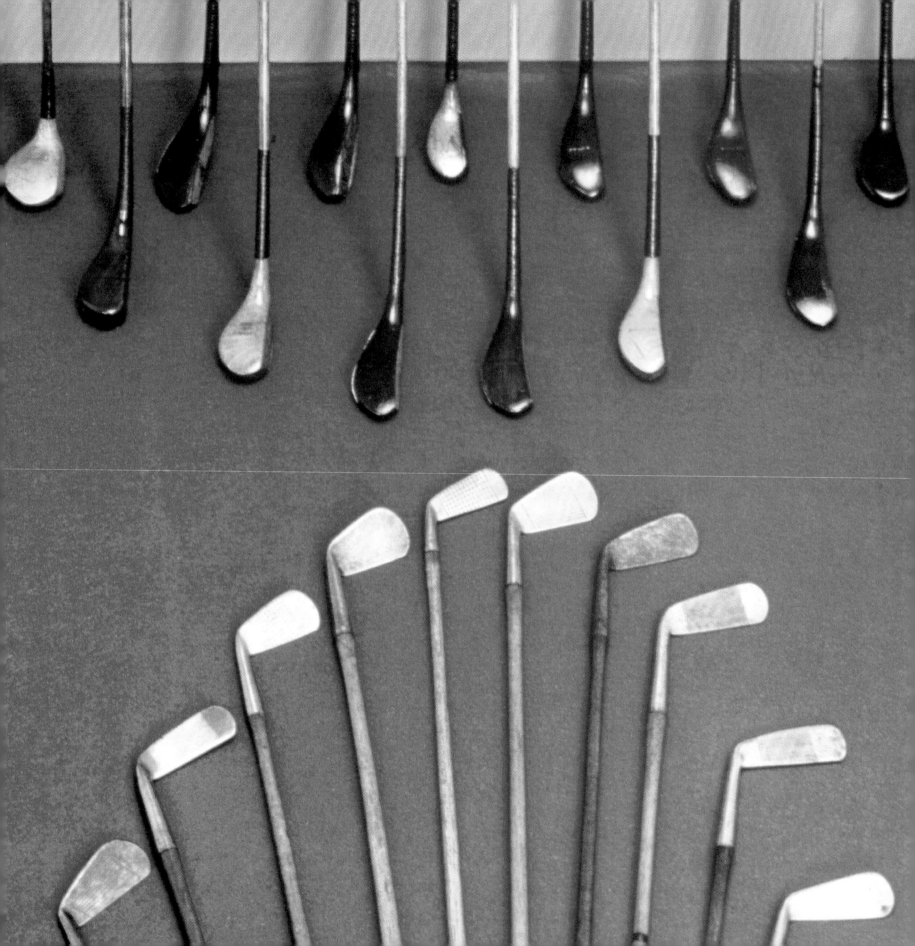

The biggest wallop was packed by the play club, a long-nosed weapon with little or no loft in its tiny, one-inch-high hitting area. Its shaft was forty-five inches long, about the same as today's drivers, but it met the clubhead at an angle of 120 degrees, forcing the early golfers to stand well away from the ball and contributing to the flat, around-the-body, sweeping swing. The sole of the clubface was reinforced with the most exotic of materials, a strip of ram's horn.

A variety of lofted woods — called spoons, because their faces were curved like the bowl of a spoon to create loft — were used for approach play, from the long spoon for distance shots to the baffing spoon for raising the ball from poor lies and over hazards. Putters were also made of wood, and a single golfer might carry as many as three of them: In addition to the traditional putter for holing out, there was the driving putter for hitting low tee shots into the wind and the approach putter for bumping the ball in to the green. All of the putters were lofted, at least in part to limit the time the ball was in contact with the unmanicured fairways and greens of the day.

Iron clubs, being hazardous to the health of the feather ball, were few and reserved for only the direst of circumstances, as suggested by their names: bunker iron, rut iron, and track iron. Their heads were bizarre-looking things with concave faces and snubbed-off toes that suited the nasty assignments for which they were intended. Since Allan Robertson and his contemporaries had little expertise in metalworking, the heads were forged in blacksmith's shops and then supplied to the clubmakers, who riveted them to the wooden shafts.

But as the ball changed, so did the clubs. The gutty was much harder than the feathery and it yielded very little at impact. When the traditional wood clubs made forceful contact with the gutty they tended to split and crack. Something had to give, and it was, of course, the clubs, which began to appear with shafts of a softer wood — hickory — imported from American forests. The new shafts also had less torsion: The clubhead lagged less far behind the hands during the

Above: Odd-looking iron clubs were devised to aid escape from the direst trouble.

Opposite: The first woods, known as play clubs and spoons, had long, shallow heads, while the irons and putters of the hickory era were simple blades.

downswing, which would eventually lead to a change in swing technique to a more up-and-down attack on the ball.

The clubheads changed also, to a softer beechwood to better absorb the hit, and became shorter and thicker to pack more punch directly behind the ball. Strips of leather were inset in the clubface, which otherwise became worn and dented from constant collision with the gutty. The ultimate effect of all of this was to lessen the strain on the weakest part of the club, the spliced area just above the clubhead.

Meanwhile, iron clubs came into their own. No longer a menace to the ball, they became the preferred implements for approach shots of every kind. Indeed, such was the growth in demand for irons that several Scottish blacksmiths abandoned their other areas of trade and took up clubmaking full-time, under the title "cleekmaker." The cleek — equivalent to the modern 2- or 3-iron — was the first to appear and was followed swiftly by the progressively more lofted mid-iron, mashie, and niblick. All of which eventually led to perhaps the most practical invention of all — a simple sailcloth golf bag.

One of the first bags is said to have been constructed by Bryant Andrews, the keeper of the clubhouse at Westward Ho!, the old links course along the southwest coast of England. Andrews, a former sailor and sailmaker, sewed some pieces of sailcloth together, figuring that the "circular shape would have the effect of enclosing the greater part

Left: The assembly line at an early cleekmaker's shop.

Right: Among the best known crafstmen was Tom Auchterlonie of St. Andrews.

of the clubshafts and thus preventing the grips from getting wet." The golf bag made its commercial debut in England in 1891; called a "carrier," it usually came fitted with a stake or arrangement of legs so it could stand or lean on its own.

Allan Robertson embraced the new irons both as a craftsman and a player, and was probably the first to master the run-up shot with a cleek. At St. Andrews, in September 1858, he ran his approach onto the eighteenth green, then rolled in his gutty for a birdie and a total of 79, making him the first man to break 80 on the Old Course.

A year later, Robertson fell sick with hepatitis and died at the age of forty-four. Among the tributes to him: "They may toll the bells and shut up their shops in St. Andrews, for their greatest is gone."

Robertson's death left a void at the top of professional golf, and in short time there was an urge to fill it. By now, the game had spread sufficiently through Scotland to produce a group of highly skilled players, with Tom Morris and Musselburgh's Willie Park leading the pack. At the same time, expanded rail travel had brought the top players and courses within easy reach of one another.

So in 1860, the Prestwick Club, on the west coast, took the first step by announcing a championship for professional golfers. To the winner they offered a unique prize, a red Moroccan leather belt embroidered

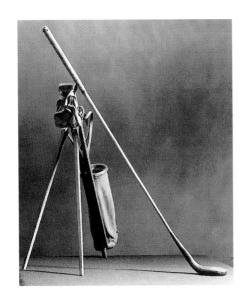

Above: Stand-up golf bags have been around for more than a century.

Below: Willie Park, putting here at St. Andrews, was the first British Open Champion.

Opposite: Old Tom Morris watches the action at Prestwick, site of the first twelve Opens.

Above: First prize was a red leather belt, embossed with silver medallions. Young and Old Tom Morris (right) combined to win eight of the Prestwick Opens.

Opposite: The belt retired with Young Tom when in 1870 he won the title for a third straight time.

with silver medallions. Permanent possession of the belt would go to whomever was capable of winning the title three years in succession.

Only eight men entered that first event, and the lowest score among them came from Willie Park with 174 for 36 holes, a rather high total even for those days. Tom Morris was next at 176 over the twelve-hole, 3,803-yard circuit. In fact, the scores were so high that a number of amateurs felt they might do better, and so the next year the competition was opened to all, and it has remained just so—the Open Championship or, as Americans know it, the British Open.

Tom Morris won the title the following year and he and Willie Park would split seven of the first eight, with Morris taking four and Park three. (The tournament was played at Prestwick from 1860 to 1872.) When Morris won for the last time, in 1868 at the age of forty-six, he became, and still remains, the oldest British Open Champion.

One year later, the title was won by a lad of seventeen years who became, and still remains, the youngest British Open Champion. And his name also was Tom Morris. This legendary father-son duo would forever be known as Old and Young Tom.

Young Tom Morris was as wonderfully gifted a player as the game had ever seen or ever would. A broad-shouldered lad, he could hit the ball with tremendous power, making him a master of the recovery from trouble, but he was also a skillful pitcher and putter, and is credited with inventing the lofted pitch shot. In truth, his game had no weakness, as he proved by defending his title successfully in 1869 and then taking permanent possession of the belt with a third straight win in 1870. On the first hole of that 1870 Open—a monster of 570 yards— Young Tom posted a 3, a score that would be equivalent to a double-eagle today. He won the title by twelve strokes with a then-astounding total of 149, a mark that would stand for thirty-four years.

He also won numerous head-to-head matches, many for big purses, against the other great players of the day. He single-handedly beat the better ball of teams of the best players, and, often teaming with his father, played challenge matches that they nearly always won.

There was a gap in Open play in 1871 because no one came forward to offer a prize to replace the belt. Then in 1872 a silver claret jug was presented jointly by St. Andrews, Musselburgh, and Prestwick, and the three sites began a club-to-club rotation that continues today, although there are now more clubs and a less strict order of rotation.

When the competition resumed, Tommy picked up where he'd left off, winning the title at Prestwick for a fourth time. He might well have won it at least another four more times, too, had he not died suddenly at the age of twenty-four.

It is still one of the saddest tales in the game's long history. In September 1875, Old and Young Tom were playing the brothers Willie and Mungo Park in a big-money match at North Berwick, across the Firth of Forth from St. Andrews. Just as the Morrises were closing out the match on the eighteenth green, Old Tom received a telegram; he wouldn't tell his son why, but they had to leave immediately on a yacht put at their disposal by a wealthy friend. As they cut across the waves, Young Tom learned from his father that his wife and newborn had died in childbirth. It was a blow from which the young man never recovered. He played golf only twice more and then, on Christmas Eve, he passed away mysteriously in his sleep. The clinical cause of his death was likely pneumonia, but in the lore of golf, Young Tom Morris died of a broken heart. One of the largest monuments in the cemetery in St. Andrews is for Young Tom. It reads, in part: "In Memory of Tommy, son of Thomas Morris . . . Deeply regretted by numerous friends and all golfers. He thrice in succession won the champion's belt and held it without rivalry and yet without envy. His many amiable qualities being no less acknowledged than his golfing achievements . . . ."

Old Tom would outlive his son by thirty-three years, and for the last half of his life he returned to his native St. Andrews as the first resident professional to the Royal & Ancient Golf Club. With his long gray beard, tweed cap, and pipe, Tom Morris was a familiar figure to all who passed by his shop near the eighteenth green.

Opposite: Young Tom "died of a broken heart" at age twenty-four shortly after his wife and newborn died in childbirth.

IN MEMORY OF
"TOMMY"
SON OF THOMAS MORRIS
WHO DIED 25TH DECEMBER 1875 AGED 24 YEARS

DEEPLY REGRETTED BY NUMEROUS FRIENDS AND ALL GOLFERS
HE THRICE IN SUCCESSION WON THE CHAMPION'S BELT
AND HELD IT WITHOUT RIVALRY AND YET WITHOUT ENVY
HIS MANY AMIABLE QUALITIES
BEING NO LESS ACKNOWLEDGED THAN HIS GOLFING ACHIEVEMENTS

THIS MONUMENT HAS BEEN ERECTED
BY CONTRIBUTIONS FROM SIXTY GOLFING SOCIETIES

CHAPTER 3

From
Apple Seeds

One of those visitors, during the late summer of 1887, was a gentleman named Robert Lockhart. A native of nearby Dunfermline, Lockhart had emigrated to the United States but his job as a linen merchant frequently brought him back to his home soil. Lockhart had learned to play golf as a boy on the links at Musselburgh, and in 1886 he decided to introduce the game to his friends in America. So, in Tom Morris's shop, he purchased six clubs—a driver, brassie (equivalent to today's 2-wood), spoon (3-wood), cleek (long iron), sand iron, and putter—and two dozen gutta percha balls.

Lockhart had the clubs shipped to his home in New York City, and upon their arrival during the winter of 1887 he and his two sons tried them out, some say in Central Park, others near what is now the intersection of 72nd Street and Riverside Drive. There is evidence that Lockhart was questioned by the police about his unusual activity that day (the policeman actually may have taken a swing or two). Satisfied that the equipment was sound, Lockhart had it shipped up to the Yonkers, New York, home of his friend and fellow son of Dunfermline, John Reid.

Six months later, on the morning of George Washington's Birthday, 1888, Reid assembled with five other gentlemen in a cow pasture in Yonkers to give golf a try.

All six became instant converts, and although their progress was halted briefly by the notorious Blizzard of '88 they soon resumed play with frequency and fervor. In the fall of that year, they assembled at Reid's home and founded a club which, in honor of the home of golf, they named the St. Andrew's Golf Club (very deliberately inserting the apostrophe). It is that day—November 14, 1888—that historians agree with virtual unanimity is the official beginning of golf in the United States.

However, this almost certainly was not the first time golf was played in America. As far back as 1650, "colf" was mentioned in the court records of New York, which was still a Dutch colony, raising the possibility that the Dutch exported the game much farther than just across the North Sea. And, as noted earlier, wherever there were English, there was golf, including instances of play in the Thirteen Colonies before the Revolution. Ship's logs note that balls and clubs were shipped from Scotland to South Carolina in the 1740s, and evidence points to the establishment of a golf club in Savannah in the 1780s, but all vestiges of any such associations vanished during the Civil War. Numerous clubs in the U.S. trace their existence, although not their courses, back to the 1870s and 1880s before Reid and Lockhart teed it up. And to the north, the Royal Montreal Golf Club was established in 1873, followed by the Quebec Club in 1875 and a club in Toronto in 1876. Yet St. Andrew's is generally regarded as the oldest continuously operating golf club in the United States.

And so it was that John Reid became the "Father of American Golf," and his band of pilgrims became known as The Apple Tree Gang, thanks to the fruit-bearing specimen that served as their makeshift clubhouse. A wide wooden bench encircled the trunk, while in its branches the members hung their coats, their lunch containers, and a wicker basket holding several pints of Scotland's other great gift to the world.

At that time, in fact, apple trees were the defining element of the St. Andrew's course, perched as it was on a thirty-four-acre orchard overlooking the Hudson River. Indeed, so imposing were the trees that initiates to the American game of golf assumed them to be integral features of any reputable course.

An early story involves one Judge O'Brien who, having niblicked his way through his first round of golf at St. Andrew's, made a visit to the Shinnecock Hills Golf Club on the barren and windblown turf of Eastern Long Island. Upon seeing that layout for the first time, the judge declared with full confidence that it "was not a golf course at all because it had no apple trees over which to loft and play."

Below: An early ladies' day at Shinnecock Hills.

Opposite: The "Father of American Golf," John Reid of St. Andrew's Golf Club, Yonkers, NY.

Chapter opener: The first photo of golf in America at the St. Andrew's Golf Course in Yonkers, NY, in 1888.

But other courses were sprouting in America—with and without apple trees—and they were sprouting quickly. Within five years of the founding of St. Andrew's, dozens of clubs had opened, aided by a steady stream of emigrant Scottish professionals.

A standing joke of the era was the availability of a club professional's job for anyone coming off the boat with the name Willie and a sufficiently thick Scottish brogue. Willie Dunn went to Shinnecock on Long Island (where he laid out the original twelve-hole course), Willie Campbell to Brookline in Massachusetts, Willie Anderson to Apawamis in New York, and Willie Smith to Midlothian in Illinois. The tiny Scottish town of Carnoustie alone would ship more than 250 men to golf professional jobs at early American clubs. And, for the most part, they were still using and teaching the flat, St. Andrews swing.

Meanwhile, one fellow traveled the other way: Charles Blair Macdonald. The son of a wealthy Chicagoan, Macdonald sailed to St. Andrews in 1872 at the age of sixteen to study at the university while staying in the care of his grandfather. The day after he arrived, Macdonald was taken to the shop of Old Tom Morris, where his grandfather bought him a set of clubs and set him up with a locker, since juniors were not allowed inside the clubhouse of the Royal and Ancient. Within a short time, the young Macdonald was spending every spare moment playing the Old Course and listening to and learning from the great players of the day, including both Old and Young Tom.

Two years later, Macdonald returned to the States with a passion for the game and strong convictions about every aspect of it. As GOLF Magazine wrote, he "seemed to regard himself as having been ordained to spread the gospel of golf in America." Since the U.S. was devoid of courses at the time, he had to make do for fifteen years playing only on business trips to Britain. Once America got the golf bug, however, Macdonald was ready, and when, in 1894, a group of the best amateurs in the land assembled at the year-old Newport Golf Club in Rhode Island to determine a national champion, C.B. was the man to beat.

Below: Newport Country Club, site of the first U.S. Amateur Championship.

Opposite: Iron-willed Charles Blair Macdonald won the first Amateur title in 1895.

But he did not win. With a score of 189 for thirty-six holes, he lost by a stroke to one of the Newport members, William Lawrence. Macdonald later protested that a stone wall, which had cost him two strokes in the second round, was not a legitimate hazard under the Rules of Golf. (He was a stickler for the Rules, lording his knowledge of them over those who didn't know them as well, which, at the time, was just about everyone.) He also claimed that a proper championship should not be a matter of who takes the fewest strokes but should be decided in a head-to-head format.

The following month he got his head-to-head when the St. Andrew's Golf Club held a second amateur championship, this one at match play. Macdonald defeated his Newport nemesis Lawrence in the semifinals, but, after halving the eighteen-hole final match, he sliced his drive into a plowed field on the first hole of a playoff and lost to Lawrence Stoddard of the host club.

This time he argued that the result was invalid because one club may not presume to run a national championship. Macdonald's gripes were largely self-serving, but he was a man with a commanding presence — broad-shouldered, thickly-mustached, well-spoken, and humorless — and he got his points across to the right people.

Lawrence Curtis, the man who started golf at The Country Club in Brookline, Massachusetts, spoke to Henry Tallmadge, one of the founders of St. Andrew's, and they agreed to invite representatives of various clubs to form a central body that would have the authority to conduct national championships and otherwise further the interests of the game. And so in December of 1894, over dinner at The Calumet Club in New York City, the United States Golf Association (USGA) was founded.

Macdonald undoubtedly wanted to be the association's first president, but was far too contentious a character for the job. It went instead to a Newport business titan named Theodore Havemeyer, with C.B. settling for second vice-president. Although not in charge, he was in his element. As an officer of the USGA for many years, Macdonald was instrumental in drafting its constitution and did all he could to assure that the game in America was played as it was in Scotland. To that end, he pushed for a single set of Rules, getting the USGA and R&A to create a (mostly) unified code.

Below: Newport titan Theodore Havemeyer became the first USGA President.

Opposite: No individual had a greater influence on early American golf than C.B. Macdonald

Overleaf: Participants in one of the early U.S. Opens.

A year after the founding of the USGA, Macdonald got what he *really* wanted — a victory in the association's first Amateur Championship. It was held at Newport in October, having been pushed back a month so as not to intrude on a more important event, the America's Cup yacht race.

Twenty-nine gentleman golfers took part and Macdonald, more determined than ever, blazed to a 12-and-11 victory in the final match over Charles Sands, a young tennis buff who had entered the championship as a lark, having played golf for all of three months.

The next day, a much quieter cornerstone was laid when a twenty-one-year-old Englishman named Horace Rawlins fired a one-day score of 91-82—173 to better a field of nine fellow professionals and one amateur to become the first United States Open Champion. Although it is now one of the most coveted titles in golf, the U.S. Open back then was little more than an afterthought, earning its first winner a $50 gold medal and $150 in cash.

C.B. Macdonald's breakthrough was also his swan song. Although he would compete in other championships, he never won again. He would, however, have a continued and lasting influence on the game, not only as an administrator but as America's first great golf course architect. It was C.B., in fact, who coined the term "golf architect."

In 1892, he was invited to lay out a few short holes on the Illinois estate of Senator John B. Farwell. Then he laid out a few more, then a nine-hole course in the town of Belmont for a new club of which he was a founder and principal money-raiser, the Chicago Golf Club. In 1895, he unveiled a new, bold design for the new club — a seaside-type course set a thousand miles from the nearest sea — that became the first eighteen-hole course in America. Over the next thirty years he designed other courses as well, including the Mid Ocean Club in Bermuda, the Yale University course, and the original course at the Greenbrier resort, called Old White. But Macdonald's undisputed masterpiece was a layout on the eastern end of Long Island, a course that, with typical pomposity, he named The National Golf Links of America.

Macdonald poured several years of his life and

Below: At the start, golf in America was very much a gentleman's game.

Opposite: Horace Rawlins won the first U.S. Open, back then merely an afterthought to the Amateur title.

many thousands of his dollars into it, and in its rolling fairways and imaginatively contoured greens he brought to bear the full measure of his St. Andrews training. When the National opened in 1911, it set a new standard for American golf architecture, and nearly a century later it continues to rank among the top twenty or so courses in the world. Inside the clubhouse is a life-sized bronze statue of C.B. Macdonald. Legend claims he commissioned it himself and then billed the membership for it.

Whether that is true or not, C.B.'s ego was truly insatiable, and he wasn't afraid to feed it in the design of his courses. A notorious slicer, he routed the Chicago Golf Club's holes in a clockwise circle to favor the left-to-right drift of his shots. Spray the ball to the right and your worst penalty was light rough; spray it left and you were flailing through a cornfield.

Since this inequity was simply too severe, a three-word phrase made its debut in the rule book of 1899: out of bounds. Thereafter, those whose shots flew too far afield were allowed to retee the ball at a penalty of one stroke.

Below: C.B. Macdonald's masterpiece, the National Golf Links of America.

Opposite: At the Chicago Golf Club Macdonald created the first eighteen-hole course in the States.

GROUNDS OF THE

CHICAGO GOLF CLUB

WHEATON ~ ~ ILLINOIS.

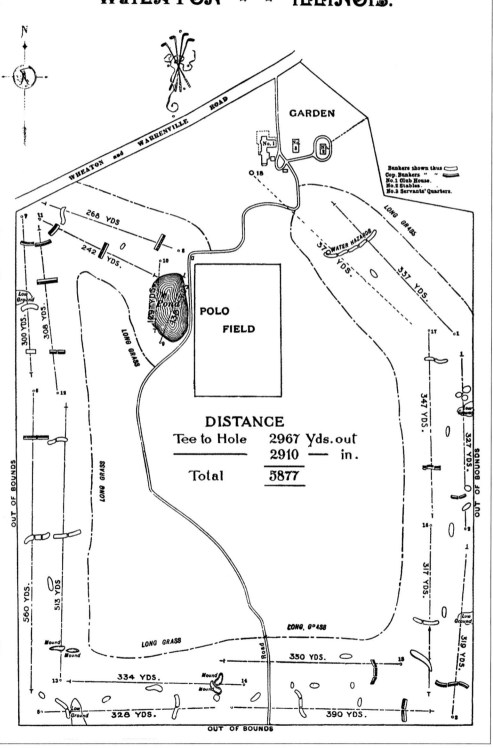

DISTANCE

Tee to Hole   2967 Yds. out
                      2910 — in.

Total   5877

CHAPTER 4

In Vardon's Grip

When the U.S. Open came to the Chicago Golf Club in 1900, one player had little fear of spraying to either side: Harry Vardon. No one had ever played golf quite like this soft-spoken stylist from the Isle of Jersey in England. He could fade it, draw it, knock it down, or loft it up, but most of all he could hit it straight—very straight. Vardon, they say, was unable to play thirty-six holes on the same day at the same course because, in the afternoon, he'd have to hit his approach shots out of the divots he'd taken in the morning!

The two players in Britain who could give Harry a game were the Englishman J.H. Taylor and

Scotsman James Braid. Collectively, the three of them won sixteen of the twenty-one British Opens between 1894 and 1914, and in each of the five years when another man won, one of these three finished second. Quite deservedly, they became known as "The Great Triumvirate." But Vardon was the greatest of the great, and in 1900 he was at the peak of his powers, with three British Opens to his credit and three more to come.

Vardon's success had numerous effects on the game, not the least of which was the transformation of the golf swing. At the end of the nineteenth century, a heated debate pitted the proponents of the flat, around-the-body St. Andrews swing against a new motion, better suited to the gutta-percha ball, which may have evolved from the open stance (body aiming slightly left of the target) employed by those adherents to the object of Britain's other sporting fanaticism, cricket. Not only did cricketeers stand open, but they employed a great deal of wrist action and made contact slightly on the upswing (rather than on the downswing as the St. Andreans did, the result of playing the ball so far back in their stance). But the most important difference was the path of the swing, which rather than rotating flatly around the torso, went up above the shoulders with the club extending to head-height. The result of all these actions was a ball that was lofted high into the air, heresy to the traditionalists who fervently believed in the low-flying projectiles of Old and Young Tom and the dozens of Willies.

But the die-hards' cause was soon dead. In 1890, Englishman John Ball won both the British Amateur and Open with an upright swing. Four years later, Taylor won his first Open by addressing the ball from an open stance and using a cricketer's motion. Then along came Vardon, whose successes were successive nails in the coffin of the St. Andrews swing.

Not only did Vardon use an upright swing, he wrote about it. While not the first golf-instruction author, Vardon was one of the first to produce best-sellers in which he described his methods in intricate detail. Here is an excerpt from *The Complete Golfer*, first published in 1905:

'Slow back' is a golfing maxim that is both old and wise. The club should begin to gain speed when the upward swing is about half made, and the increase should be gradual until the top is

Below: Upright-swinging John Ball won a British double in 1890.

Opposite: The Great Triumvirate: J.H. Taylor, James Braid, and Harry Vardon.

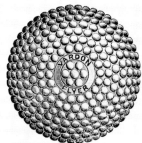

Above: The ultimate gutty was the Vardon Flyer, which Harry promoted on a tour of the U.S.

Opposite: With the success of Vardon, the wristy St. Andrews swing began to die out.

reached, but it should never be so fast that control of the club is to any extent lost at the turning-point. The head of the club should be taken back fairly straight from the ball...for the first six inches, and after that any tendency to sweep it round sharply to the back should be avoided. Keep it very close to the straight line until it is half-way up. The old St. Andrews style of driving largely consisted in this sudden sweep round, but the modern method appears to be easier and productive of better results.

And this is but a fraction of his comments just on driving. There were separate chapters on the brassie and the spoon, the cleek, mid-irons, the mashie, bunker play, and putting, as well as sections on competitive play, on caddies, on golf for ladies, and on his favorite courses, plus a few chapters of autobiography. Still, by 1921, *The Complete Golfer* (perhaps the most accurately titled golf book of all time) had gone through seventeen sold-out editions.

With Vardon at the lead, closely followed by Taylor, Braid, and the other great British players, the new upright swing took hold. In the U.S. it was championed by H.J. Whigham, a Scotsman who had been educated at Oxford, emigrated to Chicago, won back-to-back U.S. Amateurs, wooed and married C.B. Macdonald's daughter. He then wrote *How to Play Golf,* America's first great instruction book, which was published in 1897, one year after Vardon's first Open victory. Whigham was heavily influenced by Vardon's swing, and wrote in his book, "Don't, above all, as you value your golfing future, adopt a full St. Andrews swing....It is better to miss the ball in the right way than to hit it in the wrong."

Along with his influence on the swing, Vardon had a profound effect on golf commerce. His visit to America in 1900 wasn't solely to play in the fledgling U.S. Open, but was part of the game's first big endorsement contract: Equipment maker A.G. Spalding paid Vardon £900 (at a time when the prize for winning the British Open was £30) to make a nine-month-long publicity tour of the States promoting the company's hot new gutty ball, the Vardon Flyer.

For a nation newly hooked on golf, Vardon's visit was mesmerizing. Wherever he went, hundreds of people came to see at him, even in steely New York City, where Vardonmania was so fervent that on the day of his visit the Stock Exchange closed down.

They came to see just how well a golf ball could be struck, and Vardon surely showed them. During one exhibition at a Boston department store, when he became bored hitting shot after shot into a net, he spotted a protruding sprinkler valve and amused himself by aiming for it. He hit the valve so many times that the store manager begged him to stop for fear of flooding.

Vardon played more than seventy matches on his tour, winning all but about a dozen of them, a remarkable record considering that he was traveling vast distances by train, playing courses he'd never seen, and, more often than not, matching his score against the better ball of two local opponents.

In June, Harry hopped back across the Atlantic for the British Open at St. Andrews, where he finished second as Taylor won and Braid placed third. Then he returned to America and capped his triumphant tour in Chicago with a victory in the U.S. Open, turning the tables on Taylor, who finished second by two strokes.

As Vardon's amazing grace transformed the curious into converts, golf in America began a big-time boom. By the end of 1900 there was at least one course in every state—a thousand courses in all—and the U.S. boasted a quarter-million players, more than the rest of the world combined.

Not all of them were men. The first Women's Amateur Championship was held a month after the first "official" men's championship (the one finally won by C.B. Macdonald), in November 1895. Played at the Meadow Brook Club on New York's Long Island, the victor was the otherwise unknown Mrs. Charles S. Brown (her first name is lost to history, but not her husband's). Thirteen contestants vied at stroke play, and Mrs. Brown won by shooting 69-63—132—for eighteen holes! The quality improved dramatically the next year, and not only because the event went to match play. It was won by sixteen-year-old

Above: Beatrix Hoyt won three straight U.S. Amateurs, then retired in 1900 at the age of twenty.

Opposite: A determined-looking team of Princeton Tigers. Golf went to college at the turn of the century.

Beatrix Hoyt, who held the record for the youngest champion until the 1970s. Hoyt captured the amateur title in 1896, 1897, and 1898, then retired from all serious play after losing in the semifinals of the 1900 event, which was played at her home club, Shinnecock Hills.

Women were avid participants in the great American golf boom. Those in the Northeast slow to try the new game might have been pushed along by an article in *The New York Times* that began with this breathless assertion: "The woman who wants to be good and beautiful — which is to say healthy — must play golf . . . the best game ever introduced in America."

Meanwhile golf got into college, as Harvard, Yale, and Princeton fielded the first teams in an intercollegiate arena that would become the spawning ground for generations of American talent. And for one brief shining moment, the game grabbed worldwide notice when Charles Sands, the tennis-playing victim of C. B. Macdonald, resurfaced in 1900 to win the scratch medal at the Paris Olympic Games.

Yes, golf at the turn of the century was healthy. So healthy that, according to one physician, it threatened the health of its devotees. In a 1901 report, Dr. A.C. Bernays of St. Louis attributed the death of one Wayman McCreery to an overindulgence in golf. It seems the obese Mr. McCreery had shed a quick thirty-eight pounds by playing a ferocious schedule of rounds, but had died shortly thereafter. Said the doctor, "The golf fad for busy men who have become corpulent is a dangerous experiment, and the sad example of Mr. McCreery must be a warning for all."

Undaunted, Americans took to the links with Yankee tenacity. They didn't simply want to play, they wanted to play with the graceful pivot, dazzling footwork, and overlapping grip that Harry Vardon had made famous. The result was an avalanche of magazines and books on golf

technique. At the forefront of both the writing and playing worlds was the aforementioned H.J. Whigham and one Walter J. Travis.

Travis, an Australian-born American who took up the game at the age of thirty-five, won three of the first four U.S. Amateur titles of the twentieth century (1900, 1901, and 1903) decked out in a tweed cap, jacket and tie, and knickerbockers, and with an omnipresent black cigar clamped in his teeth. He was a small man and a short hitter, but overcame his lack of length with a superb short game, particularly a putting touch that regularly saved his bacon while frying his opponents'. In 1904, he traveled to England and became the first overseas player to win the British Amateur, thanks in large part to a unique center-shafted putter called the Schenectady, a weapon the Royal & Ancient Golf Club found sufficiently ominous to ban immediately after his victory; it remained illegal in Britain for half a century.

Travis immortalized his methods in a book called *Practical Golf*, became the first editor of the highly influential *The American Golfer* magazine, and designed two of the finer courses in the New York metropolitan area, Garden City Golf Club and Westchester Country Club.

At the turn of the century, the game was a twenty-million-dollar-a-year business in America, with equipment sales leading the way, except, ironically, for the little pellet that had gotten it all rolling, the gutta percha ball. By the time Harry had returned home from his 1900 tour of the Colonies, the Vardon Flyer had about flown its last as another new ball—and an American-made ball at that—made its way to the tee.

Coburn Haskell was a bicycle maker, outdoorsman, horse racer, and entrepreneur. He also was the shortest hitter in his foursome at the Portage Golf Club near Cleveland, Ohio, and, like every golfer before and after him, he daydreamed of longer drives.

One day, while visiting the office of his friend Bertram Work, an engineer with the B.F. Goodrich rubber company in Akron, Haskell noticed a scrap basket full of elastic thread. Instantly he had a brainstorm: He could wind those thin strands of rubber around an inner core and make a golf ball, the same way a baseball was wound with wool thread. Such a ball would surely be more resilient and lively than a gutta percha ball.

Well, wrapping several hundred feet of elastic into a neat little sphere was easier said than done. Years later, Work described his friend's

Above: Walter Travis was a course designer, writer, editor, and winner of three U.S. Amateurs.

Opposite: H.J. Whigham wrote America's first great instruction book, *How to Play Golf.*

Above: Sandy Herd made a last-minute switch to the Haskell ball, and won the 1902 British Open.

early frustration: "He would get the thing wound about half way and then it would leap out of his hands and go bounding about the room, unwinding naturally with Haskell scrambling after it and cursing."

But Haskell stuck with his concept, eventually getting a ball wound up, and convincing Work's company to fashion a gutta percha cover for it. The result was America's first major golf invention, and perhaps the single most important contribution in the history of the game: the Haskell ball.

It flew fully twenty yards farther than the gutty, and it hit the ground running. Initially, in fact, this increased bounce and roll made the Haskell difficult to control, especially around the green, and for a time many players carried a gutta percha ball just for chipping and putting.

But, for ladies, older players, and anyone in dire need of distance, the Haskell made golf a whole different game.

After short-hitting Walter Travis used it to win the 1901 U.S. Amateur, the ball known as "Bounding Billy" was embraced by America and within a short time the B.F. Goodrich Company was mass-producing them on an automatic winding machine.

The British were more skittish, with one critic dismissing the Haskell as "the ball for a tired man." Among the most vocal opponents was Sandy Herd, a perennial contender for the British Open who, on the eve of the 1902 Championship, denounced the ball as unfit and expressed the hope that every other professional in the field would play it, as he most certainly would not.

But a funny thing happened on his way to the tee. During a practice round, Herd got a quick lesson on playing the Haskell from the appropriately named amateur ace John Ball, and suddenly Sandy changed his mind. The result was that the 1902 British Open went to Herd by one stroke over Harry Vardon, still flogging the ill-fated Flyer.

Incredibly, Herd had used the same ball for all seventy-two holes, and, just as incredibly, he had been the only player in the field to play a Haskell.

But others had had their chances. A few years earlier, Haskell had sent the ball to J.H. Taylor, hoping that one-third of the Great Triumvirate would use it in the 1900 U.S. Open. Instead, Taylor stuck with the gutta percha and finished second to Vardon. Taylor finally did try the Haskell, teeing it up for the first time on the first hole of New York's

Rockaway Hunting Club. Taylor was not a long hitter, and figured the group on the green 250 yards away was safe. His tee shot rolled past their feet as the group was holing out.

Shortly thereafter, Horace Hutchinson wrote on behalf of his countrymen, "We accept the American invention, as Britons will, of course, with grumbling, but with gratitude deep in our hearts." And so, from both sides of the Atlantic, the message was the same: Good-bye, gutty. Hello, Haskell!

The Haskellization of golf changed everything, beginning with the implements that struck the new ball.

The softer, more springy Haskell required woods with a harder hit, and persimmon became the tree of choice, with inserts of various materials adding to the smack. Iron heads were enlarged and scored with dots and grooves to help impart backspin, and clubs with extra loft were added since now the key was not simply to make the ball go but also to make it stop. Also by this time it had been learned that curving the clubface, as had been done on the early spoons and other wood-headed clubs as a way of lofting the ball into the air, was less effective than keeping the face flat but tilting it back.

Above: From its boxwood beginnings to the rubber-cored Haskell, the golf ball had come a very long way.

With the Industrial Revolution and the golf boom both in full force, clever inventors were hard at work trying to make the game easier. The Spalding company, having failed with the Vardon Flyer, introduced their first wound-rubber ball, the Wizard, in 1903; they then developed a cover of a natural rubber called balata, which adhered more securely than gutta percha to the rubber windings inside while also proving easier to control. And in 1905 Spalding developed the first true "white" golf balls: Rather than black material painted white, these started with a real white cover.

Other companies experimented with the cover's design. The early Haskell balls had a raised "bramble" pattern, the result of a lucky discovery by Chicago pro James Foulis, winner of the 1896 U.S. Open, who unknowingly put a gutta-percha-covered Haskell in a ball press and had a product that flew longer and straighter. But it soon became clear that indentations, rather than bumps, produced better results, and in 1905 England's William Taylor patented the dimpled cover. Spalding bought the American rights, and by 1930 the dimple was king.

Below: Dimples—even square dimples—helped get the ball in the air, but the biggest boost came from the invention of the golf tee.

Coincidentally, another invention made its debut within a year or two of the Haskell ball: the golf tee. For hundreds of years, players had taken a pinch of sand and a cup of water from just off the teeing ground, and, using their fingers, formed a tiny mound on which to set the ball. One of the early responsibilities of the caddie, besides carrying his player's clubs, was deftly shaping the little knob. By the turn of the century, patents were being issued for tees made of rubber, cardboard, and steel; there was even a paper tee that unfolded and doubled as a scorecard.

The wooden tee was patented in 1899 by George F. Grant, who was not only one of the first African-American golfers in post-Civil War America, he also was one of the first African-American dentists. A son of former slaves, he began working as a boy for a local dentist, then persevered against all odds to attend and graduate from Harvard Dental School with honors. His dental background is significant because, some sources say, Grant disliked dirtying his hands as he began every hole. The tees were made for Grant by a local Boston-area artisan and he gave them away to friends, but never tried to sell them.

That job fell to another dentist, William Lowell of Maplewood, New Jersey, who patented and marketed the Reddy Tee in 1920. Two deals ensured Lowell's success, at least in the short term: The F.W.

Woolworth stores placed a huge order, and Walter Hagen was sufficiently impressed to place a Reddy Tee behind his ear as he strode down the fairways in front of the galleries. But Lowell was unable to protect his patent, and, with other manufacturers entering the tee business, he closed his company in 1933.

The turn of the century was a good time for other golf gadgets, as well. The first ball "pick-ups," forerunners of the shag bag, came on the market in the early 1890s. Soon to follow were the tethered practice ball, the hand-held ball cleaner, and even an adjustable-head club. The practice putting mat was patented in the U.S. in 1906.

Advancements in clubs and balls also heated up the endless game of attack-and-defend between golf technology and course design. Up to this time, American golf architecture had been a matter of quantity rather than quality, with the demand for places to play far surpassing the talent to design them well. As an adjunct to Vardon's 1900 tour, Spalding had dispatched a chap named Tom Bendelow across America to serve as architect for anyone who wanted a course. Bendelow had no particular knowledge or training—he was a typesetter for *The New York Herald*—but he had an authentic Scottish accent and he worked cheap, just twenty-five dollars per design. He also worked quickly, perpetrating more than six hundred courses in thirty-odd years. However, with the exception of the U.S. Open course at Medinah Country Club in Chicago, most of his work was mediocre. Indeed, his modus operandi was referred to derisively as "eighteen stakes on a Sunday afternoon."

But the new and better ball required new and better courses, so architects took up their T-squares and went back to the drawing board, designing longer layouts and adding thousands of yards to those that existed.

In Pittsburgh, father and son Henry and William Fownes unveiled Oakmont, an extreme test of golf with long, narrow fairways, more than two hundred bunkers, and eighteen fiercely sloped greens that were maintained at breakneck speed. Their philosophy was simple and stern: "A shot poorly played should be a shot irrevocably lost." With Oakmont, the penal school of golf course architecture was born, and a wave of defiant American courses would follow.

Meanwhile, golf's first top-notch resort course began to take shape when, in 1901, Donald Ross emigrated from the links of Royal

Below: William Fownes was among the first to strike back with harder courses.

Above: The bunkers of Oakmont were furrowed with heavy, saw-toothed rakes.

Below: Donald Ross was one of many Scottish pros who came to the States.

Opposite: At Pinehurst Ross designed the first grand resort course in America.

Dornoch in northern Scotland to the sandhills of North Carolina and started work on his masterpiece, Pinehurst Number 2.

About the time that the St. Andrew's club was being established in America, Ross, the son of a stonemason, was apprenticed to club-maker Robert Forgan in St. Andrews, where he fell under the spell of Old Tom Morris. After a few years, Ross returned to Dornoch, where he served as the professional and greenskeeper. In 1899, he joined the tidal wave of Scottish pros sailing to America, landing a pro's job at the Oakley Country Club near Boston, where he rerouted the course layout and met James W. Tufts. The wealthy philanthropist (he made his money building soda fountains) was planning a ten thousand-acre resort in North Carolina, to be designed and landscaped by Frederick Law Olmsted, the architect of New York's Central Park. Tufts convinced Ross to become the winter pro at Pinehurst, which would quickly become the first grand resort in this country, largely because of its golf. In time, there would be eight courses at Pinehurst, but the best of them remained No. 2, Ross's first true design, which he "finished" in 1903 but continued to refine for the next thirty years.

Ross was only slightly less prolific than Tom Bendelow — he is credited with more than five hundred courses worldwide — but far more

successful at crafting quality among the quantity. Once Pinehurst No. 2 opened he was in demand, so much so that he couldn't possibly visit every course he had committed to. Despite traveling extensively and keeping a large staff very busy, he sometimes saw nothing of a planned layout's terrain except photographs and topographic maps. But even from hundreds of miles away, Ross and his designers drew up courses that featured an emphasis on well-placed approaches and short shots, elevated greens surrounded by menacing slopes, and a deceiving subtlety—all trademarks of his beloved Dornoch. The best-known Ross courses, all still ranked among America's best, include Seminole in Florida, Oakland Hills in Michigan, Scioto and Inverness in Ohio, and Oak Hill in upstate New York.

While Ross was making his mark, a Philadelphia hotel owner named George Crump became obsessed with constructing the hardest golf course in the world. With the assistance of English architect H.S. Colt he did just that in the pine barrens of southern New Jersey, with the creation of Pine Valley. Every fairway and green on the course was set off by the sand and scrub that characterized the region. As such it was a relentless island-to-island examination in shotmaking and strategy. When Pine Valley opened in 1913, other designers, including Ross and Macdonald, hailed it as the finest course in America, and, astoundingly, it has remained that way. In the most recent update of GOLF Magazine's "100 Best Courses in the World," Pine Valley ranks number one.

Three other Philadelphians would also leave indelible marks on golf course design. The most colorful was Albert W. Tillinghast. The pampered only child of wealthy parents, "Tillie" didn't work until he was in his thirties, when he stumbled into course design. It was quickly obvious that he had a gift, which he presented mostly in the East, with Winged Foot, Bethpage Black, Baltusrol, and, in one of his few jaunts west, San Francisco Golf Club, his lasting monuments. Like Macdonald before him, Tillie's introduction to golf was a trip to St. Andrews as a young man, where he, too, was taken under the wing of Old Tom Morris. He proved a good enough golfer to qualify for the U.S. Amateur several times between 1905 and 1915, where he befriended, and lost to, the best golfers of the day. Unlike Ross, Tillinghast was intimately involved with the design and construction of his courses,

Above: George Crump sought to design the world's hardest course, and did just that, at Pine Valley.

Opposite: An early view of the par-three fifth hole at Pine Valley, "where only God can make a three."

Overleaf: Hole number four, The Inverness Club (pp. 82–83); hole number nine, Winged Foot Golf Club (pp. 84–85). Both courses bear the touch of A.W. Tillinghast.

wearing a three-piece suit and carrying a shooting stick as he tramped through the mud and brush to locate the perfect spots for tees and greens. His design work earned him millions, which he used to further promote his image, but he had neither enough money nor work to survive the Great Depression. After a short, unsuccessful attempt at selling antiques in Beverly Hills, he died nearly penniless in his daughter's house in Toledo, Ohio, in 1942.

George C. Thomas's road to golf architecture began in a flower garden: He was an authority on breeding roses. Also raised in wealth, Thomas had the luxury of studying the best designers of his day at close hand, working on a project or two with both Tillinghast and Ross, and watching his Philadelphia friend George Crump build Pine Valley. In 1919 he moved to the more rose-friendly climate of Southern California, where he built two dozen courses, notably Riviera, Bel-Air, and the North Course of the Los Angeles Country Club. In 1927, he published *Golf Architecture in America: Its Strategy and Construction,* one of the most important books in the field. After that, however, his interest in design waned and he turned to other pursuits.

Hugh Wilson stayed in Philadelphia, where he was a member of Aronimink Golf Club (which was designed by Ross and reworked by Tillinghast) and the Merion Cricket Club. In 1910, the members of Merion sent the thirty-year-old Wilson to Britain to study the great courses; after seven months abroad, he returned full of ideas, which he turned into the masterful East Course in 1912. He built the West Course two years later, built one more course on his own, did some remodeling to Pine Valley, and died young in 1925. Wilson had been aided by William Flynn (a native of Massachusetts who adopted Philadelphia as his home), who went on to design a few great courses including Cherry Hills and the Philadelphia Country Club, as well as remodeling The Country Club and Shinnecock Hills.

From the beginning, the courses created during the so-called "golden age of architecture" were more playable and enjoyable than their predecessors, not solely because of their design, but because of the advent in 1913 of the power mower. Suddenly, fairways and greens could be maintained swiftly and meticulously, while at the Old Course in St. Andrews the trusty four-legged agronomists were at last relieved of their duties.

Below: Interested spectators at the Merion Cricket Club, designed by Hugh Wilson.

Opposite: George C. Thomas's finest creation, Riviera Country Club.

CHAPTER 5

The American Revolution

That same year — 1913 — Harry Vardon returned to America for another barnstorming visit, and this time he brought along a formidable sidekick, Englishman Ted Ray. The complete opposite of Vardon in both physique and technique, Ray was a bulky, blustery, round-faced fellow with a pipe permanently clenched in his teeth, a long tweed jacket flapping behind him, and a crushed fedora perched precariously atop his head. He was a man built for power, and he used every ounce of it, with a lumbering swing that heaved and swayed and usually knocked off his hat. But when he set sail with Vardon, Ray was a fine enough player to be the defending British Open Champion.

Side by side they looked like Sherlock Holmes and Dr. Watson, and they teamed just as cleverly, winning all but one of the countless matches in their thirty thousand-mile tour.

But Harry Vardon and Ted Ray had not come to America simply to play exhibition matches. Their "solemn mission," reported *The New York Daily News,* was "to win the U.S. Open."

By this time, America's Open Championship had become a major event, not only with the many fine players who had migrated from Britain but with the increasingly talented home-breds, led by two-time defending champion Johnny Mc-Dermott (the first American to win his national championship, in 1911) and four-time U.S. Amateur champ Jerry Travers.

Nonetheless, in 1913 Vardon and Ray were still the class of the field, and the Open wanted them just as badly as they wanted the Open. In fact, the USGA had changed the dates of that Championship from early June to mid-September just so the two Brits could work it into their schedule.

When Vardon and Ray arrived at The Country Club in Brookline, Massachusetts, they were met by the largest field the Open had yet attracted. The USGA had beaten the bushes, particularly in the Northeast, for players to come out and compete, and had snared a starting group of 165. Of course, most of those players were long shots. And one of the longest was a young fellow named Francis Ouimet.

A twenty-year-old salesman with a local sporting goods store, Ouimet had grown up across the street from the Brookline course and had caddied there since the age of eleven. Although known as a fine player locally (he had won the Massachusetts Amateur), he was unknown outside of his home state, and had entered the Open with great diffidence. His main hope was to get a close-up look at Vardon and Ray.

He got that and much more. Going about his business quietly and unobtrusively, with his ten-year-old caddie Eddie Lowery at his side, Ouimet played his way into a surprising first-place tie with Vardon and Ray with one round to go. Then, after stumbling to the turn in 43 strokes, he roared home in 36 to tie them once again, forcing an eighteen-hole playoff. The next day, in a display of extraordinary cool under pressure, the young David slew both Goliaths, beating Vardon by five strokes and Ray by six.

The game of golf had never seen anything quite like it. Visiting columnist Henry Leach was incredulous at what he'd witnessed, and his report for *The New York Times* must have made readers wonder what had happened to British understatement. "When we have discovered perpetual motion, when we know the secrets of life after death, and when we may go for weekend golfing trips to Jupiter and Mars—perhaps then I will believe that your little Francis Ouimet has won today…This was the greatest day in all golf history. There will never be another like it. There cannot be."

In Ouimet, the first amateur to win the U.S. Open, America at last had its own bona fide golf hero, a soft-spoken, self-effacing young man who, despite coming from modest means, had all the marks of a gentleman. He didn't drink, he didn't boast, he didn't cuss as many of the amateurs and most of the pros did. And there was a gentleness about Francis that endeared him to all.

While being paraded around Brookline on the shoulders of the delirious fans, he leaned over to speak to a small woman, "Thank you, Mother," he said. "I'll be home soon."

The 1913 U.S. Open was not the end of the Ouimet story, although it certainly would have been more than enough for most men. He never won the Open again. The best he did was a fifth-place finish the next year and missing a playoff by one stroke in 1925. However, he did win the 1914 and 1931 U.S. Amateur titles, and served on nine consecutive Walker Cup teams, made up of the best American amateurs, who battled the best amateurs from Britain every two years, acting as non-playing captain for the last four. And, perhaps most im-

Above: America's first golf hero, Francis Ouimet on the shoulders of his jubilant fans. His young caddie, Eddie Lowery, is in the foreground.

Above: Joyce Wethered dominated women's amateur golf in the 1920s.

Opposite: Glenna Collett Vare was America's finest woman player of the same era.

pressively, in 1951 he was named the Captain of the Royal and Ancient Golf Club of St. Andrews, the first American so honored.

But in 1913, Francis Ouimet showed his country that anyone could get into golf and learn to play it masterfully, and a generation of schoolboys, caddies, and working men would follow his lead. In the decade after Ouimet's victory, golf participation in the United States grew from 350,000 to two million, and Americans became the best players in the world.

American dominance was slower to evolve among the women because the British cause was championed by Cecil Leitch and Joyce Wethered. Charlotte Cecilia Pitcairn Leitch won twelve national titles between 1912 and 1926 — five French Opens, four British Ladies', two English Ladies' Amateurs, and one Canadian Ladies' Open (in which she was fourteen holes up halfway through the thirty-six–hole final). She was one of the first women to play with power, forcefully punching the ball low, long, and strong, the way the men did.

In 1920, Leitch reached the final of the English Ladies' Amateur only to face the little-known Wethered, who had entered the tournament on a lark. Down by six holes with sixteen to go, Wethered came back to take the lead with four holes to play, eventually winning 2 and 1. She won the event the next three years, while winning four British Ladies' Amateurs between 1922 and 1929. Like Lady Margaret Scott three decades earlier, Wethered benefited by having a golfing brother (Roger, one of the leading British male amateurs of the twenties), who taught her to hit the ball hard. But she was better known for accuracy with all clubs, firing her fairway woods and long irons as straight as most good players hit their short irons. Wethered also was one of the first players to think about the mental side of golf. She had enormous powers of concentration, and forty years before Jack Nicklaus made the method famous, recommended "visualizing the shot" as part of the pre-swing routine. But perhaps the ultimate compliment paid to Lady Heathcoat-Amory, as she was later known, came from no less an authority than Bobby Jones, who said she was the best golfer, man or woman, he had ever seen.

Flying the Stars and Stripes was Glenna Collett Vare, who was the best American woman of her generation, winning a record six U.S. Women's Amateurs between 1922 and 1935. Her first taste of success

Above: Sisters and U.S. Amateur Champions, Harriot and Margaret Curtis are immortalized in the biennial Curtis Cup matches.

came in 1921 when, at eighteen years old, she beat thirty-year-old Cecil Leitch in an eighteen-hole match. After that, she went on a tear, winning countless amateur titles in the U.S. as well as two Canadian Amateurs and the French Championship. No woman in the States was a match for her. However, her single frustration was in never winning the British Amateur, having the bad luck of facing, and losing to, Joyce Wethered more than once. Their final in the 1929 British Ladies' Amateur is still regarded as one of the best matches in women's golf history: Vare was 5 up after the first nine holes, but only 2 up after eighteen. After lunch, Wethered won six of the first nine holes, but Vare fought back gamely, cutting the lead to 2 before losing on the penultimate hole. Vare's strength was a smooth, rhythmic swing that produced long, straight shots. In her honor, the award for the lowest scoring average on the LPGA Tour each year is called the Vare Trophy.

Three other American women of the twenties deserve mention. The first two were the sisters Harriot and Margaret Curtis, each of whom won the U.S. Women's Amateur (Harriot in 1906 and Margaret in 1907, beating her sister). In 1905, they were among eight players who crossed the sea to play in the British Women's Championship. Before that event began, the Americans played an informal match against a team of British women, the first time the two sides competed against each other. It took a few years, but the matches were formalized in 1932 with the first Curtis Cup, held every two years between amateur teams from the U.S. and Britain/Ireland. The sisters, for whom the matches are named, were instrumental in getting things started. The Cup matches also provided a measure of satisfaction for Vare, who was on the first six Curtis Cup teams, captaining three of them, and over that stretch the U.S. team went undefeated.

The other prominent American woman was Marion Hollins. While an excellent golfer—she won the 1921 U.S. Women's Amateur and captained the first Curtis Cup team—it is her accomplishments off the course that are even more impressive. She helped found and finance one of the first women's-only clubs, the Women's National Golf and Country Club on New York's Long Island. In the early days of golf in America, men were loath to share their courses with their wives and other women, who had to build their own. A handful succeeded, achievements that couldn't be over-appreciated in those pre-feminist days.

But Hollins's other feat may have had a longer lasting effect on the game. In the mid-1920s, she moved from the east coast to the west to work at a new club called Cypress Point. While there, she hired an architect named Alister Mackenzie to design a course on that magnificent piece of Pacific seaside. Besides being one of the country's best layouts, Cypress Point proved the catalyst for a fateful partnership of the 1930s, when Dr. Mackenzie would team up with Bobby Jones to build that great champion's dream layout. Hollins also hired Mackenzie to design a course on land she bought a few miles north of the Monterey Peninsula. Pasatiempo, in Santa Cruz, became another Mackenzie masterpiece, and the place he chose to settle down. Unfortunately, Hollins lost most of what she'd worked for in the Depression, but she was among the first to break the game's gender barriers.

Led by the likes of Wethered, Vare, and Hollins, women golfers were gaining respect. However, class-consciousness was still prevalent in golf, particularly in America and particularly with regard to professionals. The early club pros, most of them transplanted Scots, were viewed as little more than golf-talented artisans, meant to repair clubs, give lessons, and otherwise stay out of the way. But as more and more home-grown players became professionals, the spirit of American egalitarianism began to take hold.

And so in January 1916, at the Taplow Club in New York City, the Professional Golfers Association of America was formed. Its founding purposes were to set standards for golf professionals, give the pros a voice in the selection of tournament sites, and match qualified pros with the growing number of club jobs opening in America.

The guiding light was Rodman Wanamaker, heir to one of the country's leading department-store fortunes, who bankrolled the group and donated a trophy for the first PGA Championship, held in October of that year at the Siwanoy Golf Club just north of New York City. It was an unremarkable event. Only thirty-one men entered, and the Wanamaker Trophy went to England's Jim Barnes, a long-hitter who won the match-play final by a score of 2 and 1 over St. Andrews-born Jock Hutchison. However, with this event organized professional golf in America was off and running on what would become a long and extremely lucrative road.

Still, in those early days the riches of modern pro golf could not have been imagined. There was no such thing as a PGA Tour — just a few winter events in Florida — and no one would have dreamed of making a living solely by playing golf.

No one, that is, except Walter Hagen. Remarkably, he had made a prominent debut in the 1913 Open — Francis Ouimet's Open. Hagen was twenty years old, the same age as Ouimet, but there the similarities ceased.

Hagen, a complete unknown (the newspapers had him listed as "W.C. Hagin"), had arrived on the first tee at Brookline dressed like a playboy doing the Riviera, in white bucks, white flannel slacks, a shirt with red, white, and blue stripes, and a red silk bandana around his neck. He'd come down from Rochester, he announced to the other Americans in the field, "to help you boys take care of Vardon and Ray."

And he did just that. With five holes to play, Hagen tied the two Brits for the lead, as Ouimet struggled to catch all three of them. Then Hagen hit into trouble at the fourteenth hole and sealed his own fate with an audacious recovery attempt that failed to come off. He finished tied for fourth place, just out of the epic three-way playoff.

But there would be other days and other daring deeds by Walter Hagen, and in his own way this blustery son of a blacksmith would galvanize the world of golf just as certainly as did the quiet caddie from Brookline. As Ouimet became, rather reluctantly, America's first golf hero, Hagen became, quite eagerly, her first superstar.

The very next year, at Midlothian Country Club outside Chicago, it was Walter Hagen's name that went on the trophy as he led that U.S. Open from wire to wire for the first of what would be eleven major championship victories. In 1922 he became the first American to win the British Open, a title he would take three more times before the end of the decade.

Below: In 1916 England's Jim Barnes won the inaugural PGA Championship.

But it was in the still young PGA Championship that The Haig truly strutted his stuff, with five victories, including an unprecedented four in a row — a stretch in which he won twenty-two consecutive matches against the best professional golfers in America. His victory in 1921 made him the first American to win the title.

Hagen was hardly a stylist. A former semi-pro baseballer, he gripped the club as if it were a Louisville Slugger and lunged through impact on his shots with power to all fields. But he was fearless when in trouble, a magician from sand, and the finest putter of his time. No one was better at turning three shots into two.

His aptitude grew from his attitude, a curious blend of extreme self-confidence and nonchalance. He would march regally onto the first tee and announce, only half-kiddingly, "The Haig is here, who's going to finish second?" But he also expected to miss a few shots in each round, so when he did, he maintained his blithe spirit and doubled his resolve.

Hagen was one of the first great thinkers in golf. He specialized in finding ways of unnerving his opponents without actually doing anything improper. He had them worrying more about his game than

Left: Stylish to the finish, Walter Hagen at Royal Troon in 1923.

Above: Leo Diegel's lock-wristed putting style did not help him in his match against Hagen in the 1926 PGA.

Opposite: The victorious Haig regales all as his friend, the Duke of Windsor, prepares to present the British Open trophy.

their own, wondering not if but how he was going to beat them.

In the finals of the 1926 PGA Championship he faced Leo Diegel, one of the better pros of the day, but a perennial victim of Hagen's mind games. Early in the match, Hagen conceded some short putts to Diegel, who, being a shaky putter (he'd devised an odd putting technique, bending way over and sticking his elbows out from his sides), gladly took them. But on one of the last holes, Diegel was staring at a putt of less than two feet. He looked to Hagen for the nod, but got nothing in return. Suddenly, Diegel was scared: If Hagen wouldn't concede, he figured, there had to be something more to the little putt than met the eye. Diegel studied it from all angles, set up in his trademark stance — and missed! Hagen won the final, 5 and 3.

Even more impressive than what Hagen could do to other golfers' heads was what went on in his own. He had the rare ability to forget the shots he'd already hit and focus exclusively on the one at hand. Then, once it was hit, he would return, usually with a big smile and a wave, to the world around him. His advice has become part of every good lesson on the mental side of golf: "Don't hurry, don't worry, and don't forget to smell the flowers along the way."

To Hagen, tournaments were cocktail parties and cocktail parties were what he did best. During the last three holes of the 1919 U.S. Open, which he won, he is said to have smiled at a pretty girl on the sixteenth tee, struck up a conversation with her on the seventeenth fairway, and made a date with her as he walked off the eighteenth green.

Hagen was the first golf pro to recognize the need for showmanship, and his flamboyant game and equally flamboyant personality made him box-office magic. When not playing tournaments, he hit the road, doing hundreds of lucrative exhibitions, skimming a dollar or two for every fan he attracted. And he needed those dollars to finance his taste for life's finer things. According to his friend, golf writer Charles Price, "Walter made as much money as Babe Ruth but spent more money than the entire Yankee outfield."

On the cover of his autobiography, *The Walter Hagen Story,* was his mantra: "I don't want to be a millionaire — I just want to live like one." The Roaring Twenties couldn't have asked for a more perfect champion.

Hagen, despite his dandy dress and a penchant for hobnobbing with luminaries from Douglas Fairbanks, Jr. to the Duke of Windsor, never forgot his roots as a working man, and his greatest contribution to the game may have been his efforts to emancipate his fellow professionals from their role as second-class citizens.

Until the Hagen era, pros were barred from the clubhouses of the country clubs where they worked and competed. But Hagen saw himself as the best, and felt he deserved to be treated as such. If a club shut him out, Sir Walter would simply ensconce himself in the parking lot, where his butler served him oysters and champagne in the back of a chauffeur-driven limousine.

When this absurd situation became sufficiently embarrassing, clubs began to relent, and the dam officially burst at the 1920 U.S. Open at The Inverness Club, where all the competitors were welcomed to use the facilities. Hagen and his fellow pros showed their gratitude by presenting the club with a cathedral chime clock inscribed with a four-line poem:

God measures men by what they are
Not what in wealth possess
This vibrant message chimes afar
The voice of Inverness.

By June 1927, Hagen had won two U.S. Opens, two British Opens, and four PGAs. No professional golfer on either side of the Atlantic commanded more respect. And so it was fitting that, when a seed merchant named Samuel Ryder established a competition matching the best pros from America against their counterparts from Great Britain and Ireland, the U.S. captain was Walter Hagen. In fact, The Haig captained America's first six Ryder Cup Teams, competed on five of them, and won eight of the ten matches he played.

Those early Ryder Cups were as closely contested as the big-time battles today between the U.S. and Europe, but there was not nearly the same degree of public interest, at least not among Americans. One reason: The allure of any golf competition in those days was limited if it lacked the presence of a fellow named Bobby Jones.

Opposite: Hagen took the PGA title five times, including an unprecedented four in a row.

CHAPTER 6

The Ultimate Amateur

He was only fourteen years old when he burst upon the national scene in the 1916 U.S. Amateur at Merion, but even then the name Robert Tyre Jones, Jr. was well known throughout his native Georgia. A year earlier he had shot a course-record 68 at his home club—the East Lake Country Club in Atlanta—where he had been the club champ at age twelve. Then, just two weeks before heading north, he had beaten a field full of men twice his age to become the Georgia State Amateur Champion. Bobby Jones was a certified prodigy.

At Merion, Jones made his way through two matches before losing to the defending champion, Bob Gardner, while captivating everyone with his long drives, crisp irons, and fearless assault on the course. Even the hard-bitten old campaigner Walter Travis was impressed. When asked how much room for improvement the young lad had, Travis stroked his white beard and said "Improvement? He can never improve on his shots, if that's what you mean. But he will learn a great deal more about playing them."

In those days, Jones's only weakness was a terrible temper. He was prone to fits of extreme anger, cussed like a dock worker, and threw clubs at the smallest provocation. In time, however, he learned to control his competitive fire, and then flourished one of the grandest careers in the history of sports.

Within a period of eight years, from 1923 to 1930, Jones won four U.S. Opens, three British Opens, five U.S. Amateurs, and one British Amateur — a total of thirteen national championships, 62 percent of those he entered. Of his last twelve Opens — nine in the U.S. and three in Britain — he won seven, and in four of the other five he was runner up. No player before or since has come close to matching such a phenomenal record.

What is all the more astounding is that Jones compiled that record while playing no more golf than the average duffer. An amateur to the core, he put his family first, then his business as an attorney, and finally golf. He hated practice, going months at a time without picking up a club, and, in some years, the only tournaments he played were the national championships he won.

Bobby Jones was a supremely natural player, a golf genius. While others, even some of the best players, hit doggedly at the ball, Jones swept serenely through it with a broad, rhythmic swing whose lazy grace belied its power.

He was not a big man — just five-foot-nine and 175 pounds — but he was among the longest hitters of his time. His tee shots averaged 250 yards — with a hickory-shafted driver — and for decades he was the only man ever to get home in two at the seventeenth hole of the Olympic Club in San Francisco, a par five of 603 yards. But Jones's true strengths were his surgically accurate irons and his touch with Calamity Jane, the simple blade putter he used throughout his career.

Opposite: Jones won thirteen national titles in a span of eight years — 62 percent of those he entered.

Left: Jones's Grand Slam remains the most impressive achievement in the history of the game.

Opposite: It earned him a ticker-tape parade through the canyons of Manhattan.

Jones had already established himself as the best golfer in the world when, in 1930, he did the unthinkable. He won the Open and Amateur titles of America and Great Britain, all four national championships, in the span of one astonishing season, a feat *The New York Sun* christened "the impregnable quadrilateral." Ever since, it has been known as golf's "Grand Slam." Nearly seventy years later, it remains the most extraordinary achievement in the history of the game.

It was a journey that stretched across four months and several thousand miles, beginning in St. Andrews, Scotland, with the title Jones most wanted to win, the British Amateur. Victory here involved a grueling series of eight matches, and the path wasn't easy, as in three of those encounters Bobby squeaked through by the narrowest 1-up margin. But in the thirty-six–hole final against England's finest player, Roger Wethered, brother of Joyce and winner of the 1923 British Amateur, Jones won by a convincing seven holes up with six to play.

Two weeks later, at Hoylake, Jones took the lead after thirty-six holes, broke the competitive course record for seventy-two, and won his third British Open by two strokes over Leo Diegel and Macdonald Smith. No American had ever won both of these titles, back to back or

Left to right: Red
Grange, Jack
Dempsey, Babe
Ruth, Bill Tilden,
and Ty Cobb were
among the heroes
of the 1920s, but
Jones was revered
above them all.

otherwise, and on his return to the States, New Yorkers gave their conquering hero a ticker-tape parade.

Then he was off to Minnesota and the U.S. Open at Interlachen Country Club, where a 68 in round three put him in what seemed to be the driver's seat with a five-stroke lead. In the final round, however, Jones double-bogeyed three of the four par-3 holes, allowing Mac Smith to again give chase. But in a display of the competitive resilience that was his trademark, Jones finished with birdies on three of his last six holes for a two-stroke victory. The clincher was a dramatic forty-footer at the seventy-second green.

By this time a victory in the final leg, the U.S. Amateur, seemed preordained, especially since the tournament had returned to Merion, the site of Jones's national championship debut. And that is exactly the way it played out. Bobby won the qualifying medal for lowest score, was never down to an opponent in any of his matches, and, in the thirty-six–hole final, beat Eugene Homans by a score of eight up with seven holes to play.

On that day, a unit of fifty Marines in full dress was assigned to escort Jones as he played his way through a throng of eighteen thousand well-wishers, but even the Marines could not suppress the universal joy at Merion's eleventh green when Bobby completed his triumphant journey.

Bobby Jones might have been an object of intense envy had he not also been the epitome of modesty and grace. A genuine Southern gentleman, he was highly educated, with degrees in engineering (from Georgia Tech), English literature (Harvard), and law (Emory). He not only read books, he wrote them, and he wrote about golf just as gracefully as he played it.

At a time when America teemed with larger-than-life sports heroes—from Babe Ruth and Ty Cobb in baseball to Bill Tilden in tennis to Jack Dempsey in boxing and Red Grange in football—Bobby was revered above them all. Yet he remained humble, unaffected, and unassuming. At Harvard, Jones was ineligible for the golf team, having already matriculated at Georgia Tech, so he served as the team's assistant manager. At the time, he was the U.S. Open Champion.

He also was a man of immense integrity. In four different national championships, he called penalties on himself for minor infractions. When he was praised for this, Jones was almost indignant, saying, "There is only one way to play the game. You might as well praise someone for not robbing a bank." Jones's name was so synonymous with perfect behavior that the USGA named its highest award, for sportsmanship, after him.

Above: Jones
retired at age
28 and devoted
himself to his
family and his
businesses.

Opposite: His
number-one
venture was the
creation of the
Augusta National
Golf Club, which
opened in 1933.

Overleaf: Augusta
National, the par-
four twelfth hole.

Jones's career was as brief as it was brilliant. When he completed the Grand Slam, he was only twenty-eight, and at that point, having achieved all of his goals and more and worn himself out in the process, he retired, devoting the remainder of his life to his family and his business.

He had plenty to keep him occupied. He published three books (written with his regular traveling companion, newspaperman O.B. Keeler), designed a set of golf clubs for Spalding, and collaborated with Warner Brothers Studios on a series of instructional film shorts that co-starred the likes of Jimmy Cagney, Edward G. Robinson, Loretta Young, and W.C. Fields.

But the lion's share of Jones's energy went into the pursuit of a dream. In June of 1931, that dream began to take shape when he and a group of investors purchased 365 acres of land near the city of Augusta, Georgia. And in January of 1933 it became reality when the Augusta National, Bobby Jones's dream course, opened for play.

It was an unlikely venture at an unlikely time — about ten years late, to be exact. The previous decade or so had been the golden age of American golf course architecture, with more highly-regarded courses being built than in any two decades before or since, from Pebble Beach and Cherry Hills in the West to Inverness and Medinah in the middle of the country to Quaker Ridge and Seminole in the East. But 1933 was the middle of the Great Depression, a time when golf clubs were closing by the dozens, and that was when Jones chose to unveil his pride and joy.

The site of the course was equally unlikely, a Civil War indigo plantation that had been bought by a Belgian nobleman and converted into a horticultural nursery called Fruitlands. The rolling countryside was planted with a dazzling assortment of trees, shrubs, and flowers, with Georgia pines, azaleas, and dogwoods prominent throughout.

Alister Mackenzie, the famed Scottish architect, agreed to collaborate with Jones on the design of the course. Mackenzie had shown in his work on the spectacular Cypress Point course in California that he knew how to take magnificent land and fashion an equally magnificent place to play golf. (Jones first played Cypress Point in 1929, a year after it opened. He had traveled to Pebble Beach to compete in the U.S. Amateur — he was the defending champion — but was upset in the first round. Rather than leave, he

hung around and played Cypress Point a few times, where his admiration for Mackenzie's work was born.)

In Augusta, as Mackenzie drew the maps and oversaw the earth-moving, Jones played thousands of experimental shots from planned tees to planned greens. He had two strong desires: first, that the course have a natural look, that it rise out of the terrain rather than be stamped upon it, in a way he hoped would recall the softly rolling feel of the Scottish linksland he so loved; and second, that each hole offer alternative lines of attack, allowing a player to choose among conservative, mildly aggressive, and audacious routes from tee to green, with the reward in proportion to the risk.

When the design was finished, Mackenzie called it his finest achievement. Its generous fairways, sparse bunkering, and expansive greens gave the Augusta National a wide-open, welcoming appearance. It looked easy but didn't play that way, and that was exactly what Jones wanted.

"There is not a hole on the course where you can't make birdie if you just think," he said, "but there is not a hole where you won't make bogey if you stop thinking." Today, despite more than sixty changes, the Augusta National remains what Jones envisioned: a masterpiece of strategic design and the quintessential "thinking-man's" golf course.

Jones conceived of his course as a retreat where he and his friends could enjoy the game they loved in beautiful surroundings and with a degree of privacy. But almost immediately after the Augusta National opened, the USGA expressed interest in holding a U.S. Open there, the first U.S. Open to be held in the South. The Augusta National members were interested in the idea, but the thought of the USGA or any group moving in to run a tournament on their course did not sit well. "If we're going to hold a tournament," they reasoned, "let's hold our own."

And so in 1934, The Masters was born, with Jones as host and his Augusta co-founder, Clifford Roberts, the tournament chairman. Actually, in those days it was called The Augusta National Invitation, and that's what it was, an invitation from Jones to his old compatriots and the best of the new players, both professional and amateur, to get together for some good golf and good times. But it became something more than that the moment Roberts convinced his partner to play. Once word got out, newspapers from coast to coast blared the biggest golf news in four years: Bobby Jones is coming out of retirement!

Below: The par-four seventh hole at Augusta.

Opposite: Jones chose Scottish golf course architect Alister Mackenzie as his collaborator on the design of the Augusta National.

Jones played well from tee to green, but his chipping and putting were not what either he or the public had hoped to see. He opened with a 76 and finished the tournament at 294, in a tie for thirteenth place, ten strokes behind winner Horton Smith. That was as well as Bobby would do in any of the dozen Masters in which he played.

In the short time that he was at golf's center stage, Jones had enraptured golf fans on two continents, but nowhere more than in the city of St. Andrews, where so much of his career had unfolded, from his first embarrassing appearance in the British Open in 1921, when a stretch of poor play led him to tear up his scorecard and stomp off the course, to the Open he dominated from start to finish in 1927, to his crowning achievement in the Amateur of 1930.

In 1936, he came back to the town, quietly and unannounced, for a casual round of golf. Yet by the time he reached the first tee of the Old Course, five thousand St. Andreans were waiting to see him play. "Our Bobby is back," they rejoiced.

More than twenty years passed before Jones returned again to the "Old Grey Toun," and when he did it was for one of the most poignant occasions in sport, as he was made a Freeman of the Royal Burgh of St. Andrews, the first American so honored since Ben Franklin in 1757. By this time, at the age of fifty-six, Jones's body had been tragically wracked by a degenerative neuromuscular disease called syringomyelia. He had not played golf in years and could barely stand, but, as he accepted his honor, his heart and mind were as strong as ever.

Jones said, "I can take out of my life everything except my experiences at St. Andrews, and I would still have a rich, full life."

Bobby Jones died in 1971, leaving a legend and a legacy like no other. His longtime friend, sportswriter Grantland Rice, said it best: "Whatever any future giant of the links does to par, no one will ever replace Bobby Jones in the hearts of those to whom golf means more than a game."

Jones's spirit lives on with the annual playing of The Masters, an event that has grown by leaps and bounds since its modest start in 1934. And the biggest leap came just one year after its inception, when one of the game's most popular players, the diminutive Gene Sarazen, fired "the shot heard round the world."

Sarazen was three strokes off the lead in the final round when he came to Augusta National's fifteenth hole, a five hundred-yard par five

Opposite: The par-five thirteenth hole, one of the game's prime examples of strategic design.

with a pond just in front of the green. After a good tee shot left him roughly 230 yards from the hole, he elected to go for the green with a 4-wood. (Sarazen was playing that day with Walter Hagen, who supposedly pressed Gene to hurry up as he didn't want to be late for a date he'd made for that evening.)

In his usual no-nonsense manner, Sarazen planted his feet, positioned his club (closing the face a bit so it would fly longer and lower), and smacked briskly through the ball. It shot out on a low trajectory and dead at the flag, then cleared the pond, took one big bounce, and rolled straight into the cup for a 2—a double eagle 2. Sarazen had made up all three strokes with one glorious shot. He went on to par the last three holes and clinch a tie with Craig Wood, whom he trounced the next day in a thirty-six–hole playoff.

Suddenly, Bobby Jones's tournament had instant tradition and instant panache, and from that point on it has never looked back. Today, The Masters ranks alongside the U.S. and British Opens and the PGA Championship as one of the four most coveted titles in golf, the ingredients of the modern "Grand Slam."

With his dramatic victory, Sarazen became the first man to win each of those titles and simultaneously put the capper on a classic American success story. The son of Italian immigrants, Eugenio Saraceni had learned the game as a caddie in suburban New York, one of the thousands of kids inspired by the heroics of Francis Ouimet. When, at age fifteen, he saw his name in a newspaper for having made a hole in one, he decided "Eugenio Saraceni" looked more like the name of a violinist than a golfer, and so he changed it to Gene Sarazen.

Five years later, that name was etched onto the U.S. Open trophy when, in 1922, Sarazen won by one stroke over Bobby Jones. Later that same summer, he added the PGA title, becoming, at age twenty, the youngest champion ever. Then, in 1923, he made it two PGAs in a row.

His success may have been too much too soon, and he fell into a decade of relative decline. As he approached his thirtieth birthday in 1932, Sarazen analyzed his problems and decided that his high scores had come largely from one thing: poor play from the bunkers. So he did something about it, for himself and for the generations of golfers to follow him. He invented the sand wedge.

Opposite: Gene Sarazen put The Masters on the map when he hit "the shot heard round the world."

Sarazen had gotten the idea while flying in a plane with billionaire Howard Hughes. On takeoff, when the tail fins of the plane went down, the plane rose up. He reasoned that if he could lower the sole of his niblick (9-iron), maybe that would help lift the ball from the sand. So, working in the basement workshop of his Florida home, he soldered a thick flange on the back of the club and angled it so that the flange hit the sand first, allowing the front of the club to bounce upward. Now he could hit behind the ball and splash it out.

Sarazen was not the first to follow this notion. Bobby Jones, Walter Hagen, and Horton Smith all had sought bunker relief with variously doctored niblicks. But Gene was the first to succeed.

Surreptitiously, he brought the club with him to the 1932 British Open at Prince's Golf Club in southeast England, not unveiling it until play began, for fear the rules moguls of the Royal & Ancient would ban it (remember, they were still outlawing the center-shafted putter Walter Travis had used in 1904). Sarazen's new club worked like a charm, saving him stroke after stroke from the sand while restoring the feisty confidence of his early days. He won the title by five strokes, breaking the tournament's seventy-two–hole record in the process. Two weeks later, he won the U.S. Open at Skokie Country Club in a virtuoso performance that saw him cover the final twenty-eight holes in an even one hundred strokes—an average of 3.6 strokes per hole.

At about the same time, another major development was occurring on the equipment front. In the late 1920s, the USGA and the Royal & Ancient had approved the production of golf clubs with shafts made of tubular steel. And this blessing came not a moment too soon, since America's hickory forests had nearly been depleted by the demand for wooden-shafted clubs.

With steel, clubmaking switched from a craft dependent on the skilled eye and hand of an artisan to a purely mechanical process. The most immediate benefit was uniformity: Suddenly all clubs were created equal.

Up to this point, golfers had built up their arsenals rather haphazardly, buying a brassie here and a mashie there in hopes of assembling a collection of sticks with similar heft and flex. But, all too often, the result was a bagful of weapons that were eternally at odds with one another. Stiff shafts and whippy shafts, flat lies and upright

Opposite: With his victory in the 1934 Masters Sarazen became the first player to win the modern Grand Slam.

Above: Sarazen got the idea for the sand wedge after flying in a plane with Howard Hughes.

Opposite: In 1932 the new club spurred him to victory in both the British and U.S. Opens.

lies, heavy heads and light heads all came to roost in the same nest while their bewildered owner wondered how, on a given day, he could be "on" with one club and "off" with another.

But steel shafts put an immediate end to that with the advent of the matched set. Not only were the clubs consistent from one to the next, but the lie of the clubhead and the flexibility of the shaft could be custom-tailored to fit individual needs. There was even a mysterious new measurement called swingweight, the measure of the balance of a club's weight between its grip and head ends, that could be calibrated to a golfer's liking.

It was also at this time that golf clubs began to be designated with numerals instead of names — the spoon became a 3-wood, the mashie a 5-iron, the niblick a 9-iron, and so on — and for a while those numerals got out of hand. With no limit on the number of clubs in a set, golfers began arriving at the first tee with two dozen and more. Lawson Little, the winner of back-to-back titles in both the U.S. and British Amateurs in 1934 and 1935, is reputed to have secured his quartet of victories with the help of no fewer than thirty-one clubs.

Clearly, something had to be done, if only to save the sacroiliacs of the caddies, and so in 1938 the USGA put its foot down, limiting the golfer's armaments to fourteen. The R&A followed a year later, and fourteen remains the maximum number to this day.

Four years later another cap was imposed, this time on the liveliness of the golf ball. In the three decades or so since the invention of the Haskell, steady improvements had been made in golf-ball design and production. Back in the twenties, the game's two ruling bodies had limited the size and weight of the ball, but that hadn't stopped one manufacturer from creating a rocket that went fifty yards farther than anything on the market. What's more, as golfers began swinging their steel shafts with a slashing vigor that had been impossible in the hickory era, everyone from tour pros to grandmothers got a jolt of extra distance. So in 1942, the USGA imposed a limit on the velocity a golf ball may have at impact — 250 feet per second when measured under controlled conditions on the Association's testing device.

CHAPTER 7

An American Triumvirate

Still, as golf equipment became more consistent, more precise, and more powerful, so did golf's best players, and in the late 1930s a new breed of strong and talented professionals came to the fore.

Certainly, the game was in need of them. The retirement of Bobby Jones combined with the difficulties of the Depression had thrown big-time golf into a decade of doldrums. Although Walter Hagen and Gene Sarazen had done their best to charm the fans, their prime years had passed. Across the pond, an elegant Englishman named Henry Cotton had

Above: Byron Nelson was the first man to adapt successfully to steel-shafted clubs.

Opposite: His 1945 feat, winning 18 tournaments — 11 of them in succession — will never be equaled.

Chapter opener: Ben Hogan and Byron Nelson.

plenty of game but not much grass-roots appeal. Golf historian Herbert Warren Wind captured this pre-War drabness in one picturesque line. "Golf without Jones," he said, "was like France without Paris — leaderless, lightless, and lonely."

The professional game needed the kind of shot in the arm that only a headliner can provide, and it got not just one but three of them when America produced its own Great Triumvirate: Byron Nelson, Sam Snead, and Ben Hogan.

All three were born in the year 1912, but it was Nelson, a lanky, baby-faced Texan, who first gained major attention when he won the 1937 Masters.

He was four strokes off the lead in the final round, and the man in front was Ralph Guldahl, arguably the best player of the time. But at Augusta's treacherous par-three twelfth hole, Guldahl found Rae's Creek and took a double-bogey five, then followed with a bogey at the par-five thirteenth. Nelson, playing just behind him, birdied the twelfth and eagled the thirteenth. Against Guldahl's 5-6 he posted 2-3, picking up six strokes in the space of two holes for a two-stroke lead that he never relinquished.

Two years later, Nelson won the U.S. Open, again in dramatic style, holing a 1-iron approach shot for eagle en route to a playoff victory. That 1-iron, although spectacular, was not unexpected — not from Byron Nelson. For not since Harry Vardon had the game seen anyone hit the ball with the unremitting accuracy of Lord Byron.

His key was his swing — a swing unlike all others — the first swing to adapt successfully to the new and different demands of the steel-shafted club. Nelson, who came to the game as a caddie in Ft. Worth, was weaned on hickory, but he realized that the handsy style required for wooden shafts would not work for steel. And so, while the rest of the world continued to imitate Bobby Jones, with little leg movement and a pivot against a tall and braced left side, Nelson put some action in his legs, let his left knee buckle, and actually dipped downward through impact. However, he did continue to use one element of the swing pioneered by Jones — the straight left arm.

Until that time, all the way back to the old St. Andreans, the left arm was allowed to bend or "break down" on the backswing, something players had to do to keep their motion in sync with their wooden-

shafted clubs. But suddenly the shafts were firmer, so the leading arm could be, too. Jones was among the first to keep the left arm straight, and it helped him create power, working in conjunction with his straight, strong left side. But if Jones was the first, Nelson was the most important, for along with his other adjustments he helped popularize the "modern" swing, very similar to the one we use today.

When in form, Byron Nelson simply did not miss shots. And he was in form a good part of the time. By 1944, Nelson had added a second Masters title, the PGA Championship, and two dozen tour victories to his resume. In 1944 alone he won eight events. He had reached a pinnacle few golfers ever know, but he was about to climb much, much higher.

In 1945, Byron Nelson came as close as any golfer has ever come to being unbeatable. There were thirty-five tournaments on the schedule that year, and Nelson won eighteen of them, more than half. Even more incredibly, he won eleven of those events in one marvelous, unbroken string. To put that in context, the next longest streak by any man, before or since, is six events.

In addition, Nelson finished second seven times, and in thirty events never finished lower than ninth. His total prize money for that year of years was sixty-three thousand dollars. The same performance on today's PGA Tour would earn roughly fourteen million dollars. (Someone soon may be able to reach that, but due to the ever-increasing purses, not to a Nelson-like performance.)

It often has been argued that this season of dominance could have occurred only at a time when the best of the competition was still away at war. But in fact, Nelson's two main rivals—Hogan and Snead—played in several of those 1945 events. Besides, there was an efficiency about Nelson's performance that year that said nothing and no one could have stopped him. His scoring average for the season was 68.33—still a record—and for the year he was 320 strokes under par. Indeed, he never failed to finish a tournament that year under par.

At the end of the next season, Nelson followed in the footsteps of Bobby Jones. Exhausted by the grind and with most of his ambitions fulfilled, he retired and followed another dream, using the money he had saved to buy the eight hundred-acre Texas cattle ranch he had always wanted. In fact, along the way, whenever he would earn a good check,

Opposite: A season after his record year Nelson retired, using the prize money he had earned to buy a ranch in Texas.

Below: Sam Snead came out of the woods of western Virginia with more talent than anyone had ever seen.

Opposite: His career total of 84 victories is the all-time PGA Tour record.

he'd joke, "That's another cow," or "That's the tractor I wanted."

Years later, he returned to the game as a television commentator and as annual host of a tournament in his name. The Byron Nelson Classic, held in a suburb of Dallas, not far from his hometown of Ft. Worth, is the only PGA Tour event named in honor of a player, and that is altogether fitting, because golf never produced a finer gentleman.

Nelson retired in 1946 at the age of thirty-four. At that point, Samuel Jackson Snead was just getting warmed up. Although by 1945 he had three dozen victories under his belt, there were nearly fifty more wins ahead of him in a career that would last another thirty-four years and beyond.

Slammin' Sam, as he became known, had come out of the back woods of western Virginia with more raw talent than the game had ever seen. Although completely self taught, playing in bare feet with clubs homemade from tree limbs, Snead was blessed with a swing as strong and graceful as the leap of a panther.

In his first pro event, the 1936 Hershey Open, Sam stepped to the tee, reared back, and belted his opening drive out of bounds. He teed a second ball and hit it out of bounds, too. For his third attempt, he settled himself, let his swing flow, and drove the green, 350 yards away. With that shot, he had arrived.

Snead finished fifth in that tournament and later that year won his first event. The next year he won five more, the first installments on an eventual total of eighty-four victories, more than any man in history.

But in that same 1937 season, Snead also set himself a pattern of frustration when he finished second in the U.S. Open despite a closing-round 71 and a four-round total of 283, just one stroke off the tournament record at the time. Indeed, the single blemish on his magnificent career is his failure to win the Open despite thirty-seven tries, a dozen top-ten finishes, and an agonizing four times as runner-up. Here's a big "if," but a tantalizing one: If Sam Snead had managed to shoot 69 in the final round of each Open in which he was in contention, he would have won five times and reached a playoff in three other years.

Snead's most painful loss was to Byron Nelson in 1939 at the Spring Mill Country Club near Philadelphia where a par five on his final hole would have taken the title. Instead, thinking he needed to birdie the hole, Snead stumbled to an inglorious 8 that featured three shots from bunkers (only two got out) and a three-putt from forty feet away. "That night I was ready to go out with a gun and pay somebody to shoot me," he said later. "It weighed on my mind so much that I dropped ten pounds, lost more hair, and began to choke even in practice rounds. My doctor said I was headed for a nervous breakdown."

He had another chance in 1947 at St. Louis Country Club, where he holed an eighteen-foot putt on the final green to force a playoff with Lew Worsham. When the two came to the eighteenth green the next day, still even, both balls were about thirty inches from the cup. Snead set up to putt first, but Worsham asked for a ruling to determine the order. "That kind of rattled me," Snead said. "But it was a little bitty downhill putt with a left-to-right break. Yikes! Just the kind of putt that scared the daylights out of me." Snead was, indeed, farther away, and when he finally putted, he missed. Worsham made, for a one-stroke win.

In 1949, at Medinah, Snead needed pars on the last two holes but took three strokes from the edge of the seventeenth green and lost by one to Cary Middlecoff. And in 1953 at Oakmont, he entered the final round just one stroke behind Hogan; a final-round 76 left him six back.

But history shows that Snead recovered from his disappointments with both his composure and his game. No entry in the record book is longer than the one with his name on it: Among his seven dozen wins are three Masters, three PGAs, and a British Open, plus scores of lesser titles both at home and abroad. Some counts put the grand total at over 160 victories.

Sam Snead was the Methuselah of the fairways. Age never seemed to slow him. He won at least one tournament every year until 1962, a quarter century after he

Opposite: The single glaring omission from Snead's resume is a victory in the U.S. Open, the event where Ben Hogan excelled.

began, and in 1965 he won the Greater Greensboro — his sixth victory in that event — becoming, at the age of fifty-two years and ten months, the oldest player ever to win on the PGA Tour. Nine years later, he came within two strokes of winning again, at Los Angeles, and also tied for third in the PGA Championship — at the age of sixty-two.

But even then his competitive days were far from over. In 1979, with consecutive rounds of 67 and 66 in the Quad Cities Open, Snead shot and then bettered his age, the first and only man to perform such a feat in PGA Tour competition. And when in 1980 he won The Commemorative, a Senior event, he became the first golfer to record victories in six different decades. He will likely be the last, for Sam Snead surely was one of a kind.

While Snead played glorious golf naturally, Ben Hogan had to, in his own phrase, "dig it out of the dirt." Just five-foot-eight-and-a-half-inches tall and 135 pounds, Hogan was the runt of the caddie pen at the Glen Garden Country Club near Fort Worth: coincidentally, the same club where Byron Nelson caddied and learned the game. In fact, in 1927 Hogan lost the caddie championship to Nelson in a playoff. It was Bantam Ben's first taste of defeat, something he definitely did not enjoy.

But there was more frustration to come for Ben Hogan. For the first several years of his career, he, like Nelson and many other players before him, fought a vicious hook, and had a hard time taming it. He made three abortive attempts at the pro circuit before achieving modest success in 1937. It was another three years — and several near-misses — before he broke through with his first victory at the Pinehurst North-South in 1940. By that time, Nelson and Snead had won thirty tournaments between them.

But Hogan was about to make up for lost time. He won in each of the two weeks following Pinehurst, taking four tournaments in all, and finished the season as the leading money winner. In 1941 and 1942 he continued the domination, piling up a dozen more victories while topping the money list in both years.

Then, just as his game was reaching its peak, Hogan was called to war. He served two years in the Army Air Corps before his discharge in the late summer of 1945. Once back, he wasted no time, winning five events by the end of the year. Then, in 1946, he put together a sea-

Opposite: Just five-foot-nine and 135 pounds, Hogan worked harder — and overcame more — than any great player in history.

son that was nearly as overpowering as Nelson's the year before: Of the thirty-two events he entered, Hogan won thirteen, finished second in six, and finished third in three while competing weekly against full fields of the game's very best.

Among the tournaments he won was his first major championship — the PGA Championship — and among those he almost won were The Masters and the U.S. Open. In each of those two, a missed putt at the final hole had cost him a shot at the title.

Hogan didn't much like putting. He saw it as a game within the game of golf, a game he was never remotely able to master. But he came about as close as anyone to mastering golf from tee to green, thanks to a monkish devotion to hard work.

He claimed he preferred practice to play. Four-hour sessions on the range were not unusual for him. Once, when he noticed that his fairway woods lost some accuracy when he tired, he deliberately fatigued himself on the practice ground in order to ponder his condition and rectify it.

It was through his relentless pursuit of improvement that he banished his unruly hook in favor of a fade, which followed a safer and softer left-to-right arc that found the fairways and held the greens. Having discovered this method, he worked at making it an ingrained part of his game, hitting ball after ball until his swing repeated so automatically that one writer likened it to a machine stamping out bottle caps.

Along with the game's best work ethic, Hogan brought to golf the mind of a championship chess player. On the course he was all concentration, never smiling, almost never speaking. "Eighty percent of winning is management," he said, and he managed himself and the golf course with a ruthless rigor. His nicknames said it all: He was "The Hawk" in America, the "Wee Ice Mon" in Britain.

In 1947, Hogan again led the Tour in victories with seven, and in 1948 he added ten more, including a second PGA Championship and his first U.S.

Opposite: His repetitive swing was likened to a machine stamping out bottle caps.

Below: But his career came to an abrupt halt after an auto accident in February of 1949.

Open, won by a commanding five strokes at the Riviera Country Club in Los Angeles.

Eight months later, he was lucky to be alive. In February, after winning two of the first four events on the 1949 Tour, Hogan and his wife Valerie were driving home to Ft. Worth when his car collided, grille to grille, with a Greyhound bus that had tried to pass a truck on a foggy stretch of Texas highway. Had Hogan not instinctively flung himself in front of his wife to protect her, the steering wheel would have impaled him against the front seat. Instead, he broke his collarbone, fractured his pelvis, crushed his ankle, and suffered massive internal injuries.

Doctors said he might never walk again, much less play golf, and it was two months before, weighing ninety-five pounds, he was brought home from the hospital. But Hogan's will to win was undiminished, and he methodically drilled his body back into shape. By August he was swinging a club and by December he was on the course. The following January, he returned to the site of his Open victory, Riviera, for a comeback. Walking on legs wrapped in elastic bandages from ankle to hip to aid circulation, he shot rounds of 73-69-69-69, and, incredibly, appeared to have won the tournament before Sam Snead tied him and then prevailed in a playoff.

But Hogan was back, and if any doubters remained he convinced them that June, when the U.S. Open came to Merion. Although in visible pain from the stress of walking a thirty-six–hole final day, he managed to tie Lloyd Mangrum and George Fazio in regulation play, then beat them both the next day in an eighteen-hole playoff. His victory remains one of the most inspiring performances in sports.

Thereafter, Hogan concentrated his limited strength on the major championships, winning his first Masters in 1951 and in the same year taking the U.S. Open title at Oakland Hills near Detroit with a final-round 67 over a course setup that is still considered the most severe test ever given to the pros.

But Hogan's vintage year was 1953, a season in which he won The Masters, the U.S. Open, and the British Open within a space of twelve weeks. At Augusta, he beat Sam Snead by six strokes with a 284 total that lowered the tournament record by five. At Oakmont, he opened with a 67 and led from wire to wire, taking the Open for the fourth

Opposite: When he won the British Open in 1953, Hogan capped an unprecedented Triple Crown.

time in his last five starts. Then, persuaded to play the British Open for the first time, he sailed across the Atlantic, spent a week learning the subtleties of linksland golf, and assaulted the course and the field at Carnoustie, playing the most gratifying golf of his life. With a course-record 68 in the final round he won by four strokes.

Hogan became only the third player to win the U.S. and British Opens in the same year, and the first to combine them with a victory in The Masters. On his return to the States, he became the first golfer since Bobby Jones to get a ticker-tape parade in New York City. No player since has been so honored.

In all, Hogan won nine major championships, six of them in the years following his accident. For golfers everywhere, his name remains a symbol of courage, dedication, and indomitable spirit.

And for many it also means hope — hope of improving their own swings. Even though other professionals had written books and magazine articles passing on their magic methods, it was Hogan everyone wanted to hear from. For years, there were rumors of a "secret," something he had learned during his hours on the practice range. In 1955, *Life* magazine paid Hogan to reveal what he had learned. He confessed that he "cupped" the left wrist just before reaching the top of the backswing. In 1957, he produced what is still one of the most influential instruction books ever published, *Five Lessons: The Modern Fundamentals of Golf*, written with Herbert Warren Wind. In it, Hogan further described the "pronation" of the wrists on the backswing, something he said the old Scottish pros brought with them when they emigrated to America, as well as the importance of the left hip turning out of the way on the downswing to generate power. And he introduced a new image to the method-mad public: the pane of glass. He visualized a sheet of glass that ran from the ball up through the shoulders and indicated the proper plane of the swing. His ideas are still being debated, and tried, more than forty years later.

Opposite: He became the first player since Bobby Jones to get a ticker-tape parade.

CHAPTER 8

Ladies' Day

The era of Hogan, Nelson, and Snead transformed big-time golf into a game that was strictly for professionals. And not only for men. Within a few years, the women would also get into the act — but not right away.

The best women's play was still at the amateur level. It was 1947 before the Women's British Amateur title went to an American woman, the same woman who had won the 1946 U.S. Amateur. Her name was Mildred, but everyone knew her as Babe.

Babe Didrikson was born in Texas, just like Hogan and Nelson, and just two years after them. But well

Above: Babe Zaharias was the most gifted female athlete the world had ever seen.

Opposite: She shot ninety-three in her first round of golf, while slugging out 250-yard drives.

Chapter opener: Patty Berg and Babe Zaharias.

before Ben and Byron made their marks, the Babe was famous worldwide. Not, however, as a golfer. She had earned her nickname playing baseball in school, where, it was said, she hit home runs as often, and as long, as Babe Ruth. At the 1932 Olympic Games, she won two gold medals, in the javelin and 80-meter hurdles, and tied for first in the high jump before being disqualified on a technicality. She was a natural athlete, gifted at everything she tried—an All-American basketball player, accomplished swimmer and diver, expert rifle shot, bowler, figure skater, and bike racer, as well as a tennis player of tournament caliber. She even dabbled in baseball and football. No woman—and few men—could run, jump, throw, and hit like the Babe. She could win just about anything except the Kentucky Derby.

But golf—the last game she tried—became her one true love.

In the first formal round she played, just a few days after collecting her Olympic medals, she shot 93 while slugging out tee shots of 250 yards. In 1935, she won the first important tournament she entered, the Texas Women's Amateur Championship, in which she holed a sand wedge shot from a mud puddle for an eagle that clinched the title.

Along with her native talent, Babe brought to the sport a work ethic that women's golf had never seen. She learned the game from Tommy Armour, a U.S. and British Open Champion and the finest teacher of his time, and she worked diligently at what he taught her, playing and practicing up to sixteen hours a day. "I'd hit balls until my hands were bloody and sore," she said in her autobiography. "Then I'd hit some more with tape all over my hands and blood all over the tape."

Her first years were spent touring the country in exhibitions with the top men professionals, including Gene Sarazen, and later with her husband, professional wrestler George Zaharias. A born performer, the Babe lived for the limelight and entertained like a vaudevillian. When asked how a slender, five-foot-seven-inch woman could hit the ball so far, she said, "I just hitch up my girdle and give it a rip."

Her exhibitions made her a professional to the USGA, but by 1944

she was reinstated as an amateur, and she wasted no time in making her mark, winning the 1946 U.S. Women's Amateur at Southern Hills in Oklahoma, and then the 1947 British Amateur at Gullane, Scotland, in a performance so overpowering that one of the local scribes said, "It seems cruel to send our girls out against a game like that." In 1946–47, she claimed to have won seventeen consecutive events.

The Babe then turned pro again and acquired the services of Fred Corcoran, a well-known agent who had handled Sam Snead and baseball slugger Ted Williams. In the same year she signed a contract with Wilson Sporting Goods for $100,000.

She was making money, but what she really wanted was competition and an audience. So in 1950, to meet and exploit those needs, the Ladies Professional Golf Association was formed, with eleven women as its charter members and the Babe as its star attraction. Corcoran agreed to stage-manage the tour and Wilson paid the bills, but it was the women themselves who kept the books, wrote the checks, handled the correspondence, and even called their own rulings.

The Babe dominated those early years, winning the money title four times in a row and racking up thirty-one tournament victories, including three Women's U.S. Opens. And it is likely that she would have won dozens more events had her career not been curtailed by cancer.

She was diagnosed in 1953, and her doctor's prognosis was not good. "I don't know if surgery will cure her," he said, "but I will say that she never again will play golf of championship caliber." He didn't know the Babe. Fourteen weeks later, she was back on the course, and the next year she won five tournaments, including the U.S. Open—which she won by a whopping twelve strokes! She collected three more victories in 1955, but then the cancer returned. In 1956, Babe Zaharias died at the age of forty-two.

Babe was not the only talent on that fledgling women's tour. Even on her best days she could be beaten by a tiny (five-foot-one) freckle-faced tomboy named Patty Berg.

She came from Minnesota, an unlikely training ground for golf. Speed skating and street football had been part of her early sports activities. But by age sixteen, Patty had won the Minneapolis City Golf Championship and a year later she nearly won the U.S. Amateur, losing in the final to Glenna Collett (who was now Mrs. Edwin Vare, en

Above: Zaharias won thirty-one tournaments, including four U.S. Opens, before cancer ended her life at age forty-two.

Opposite: The Babe and Patty Berg (second row, third and fourth from the left), were two of the pioneers of the Ladies Professional Golf Association.

Above: Freckle-faced Patty Berg won fifty-five tournaments and countless fans around the world.

Opposite: Louise Suggs won the British and Women's Amateurs as well as fifty LPGA events.

route to her record sixth title). In 1938, Berg won the U.S. Amateur, which she followed with twenty-eight other amateur titles.

Berg turned professional in 1940, signed an endorsement contract with Wilson (a company she still represents), and began touring the country doing clinics and exhibitions. She won her first professional title, the 1941 Women's Western Open, then served in the women's Marines during World War II. She hit the ground running after the war with a victory in the first Women's U.S. Open in 1946. Along with Babe Zaharias, Berg dominated women's pro golf for the next decade, amassing a career total of fifty-five wins.

But Patty Berg's most important role has been as a tireless advocate for the game of golf. When the LPGA was formed she was its first President, and her service to the game has never wavered. When she won the Open she handed back the five hundred dollar check, asking officials to use the money to promote junior golf. For more than half a century, she has crossed America and circled the globe, giving clinics and talking up the game to whoever will listen. Golf has never had a better ambassador than Patty Berg.

There were many other top-notch players at the dawn of the LPGA. Louise Suggs had learned the game at age ten from her father, an Atlanta club pro, developing a swing with such blinding clubhead speed that people called her the female Ben Hogan. Before turning pro she captured numerous amateur titles, including both the U.S. and British Amateurs, then added two U.S. Opens and an LPGA Championship to her total of fifty career victories. A feisty competitor, she liked nothing more than to go head to head with Patty and the Babe. "When we're going at it in a tournament," she said, "it's like three cats fighting over a plate of fish." Just how good was Louise Suggs? When she won the 1949 U.S. Women's Open, the Babe finished second ... by fourteen strokes!

Rounding out the so-called "Big Four" of women's golf was Betty Jameson, who finished second to Patty Berg in the first U.S. Women's Open (it was a match-play event), and then won the second Open in

1947 at stroke play: Her 295 for four rounds was the first time a woman had broken 300 over 72 holes. She, too, had had a strong amateur career, beginning with a win in the Southern Amateur at age fifteen, as well as numerous Texas Amateur titles; in all, she won fourteen amateur events, topped off by the 1939 and 1940 Women's Amateur crowns. She created a strong, accelerating swing, which netted her nine victories on the nascent ladies' professional tour. She also donated the trophy for the woman with the lowest scoring average of the year, naming it after Glenna Collett Vare.

Betsy Rawls was a Phi Beta Kappa graduate of the University of Texas who didn't take up golf until her late teens. An excellent shotmaker and short-game artist, she quickly made her mark as an amateur, finishing second in the 1950 U.S. Women's Open. She turned professional the next year and won the Open a few months later. She would add three more Open titles, two LPGA Championships, and wins in forty-nine other events for a total of fifty-five victories, placing her third on the all-time victory list. Her best season was 1959, when she won ten events and the Vare Trophy. Rawls retired from competitive play in 1975, but stayed active in competition by working first as tournament director for the LPGA, and then as tournament director for the McDonald's LPGA Championship, one of the tour's four major championships.

Only one other player has won the Women's U.S. Open four times—Mickey Wright. Fittingly, when she played in her first Open at age nineteen it was 1954, the year of Babe Zaharias's final victory, and Mickey was paired with the Babe, whom she outdrove on several holes. She finished fourth that year, but in the decade that followed Mickey Wright became the undisputed successor to the Babe while setting a new standard of excellence in women's professional golf.

In contrast to the effervescent Babe, Mickey was shy and retiring. But what she lacked in glamour she delivered in game, with a swing of surpassing grace and effortless power, a swing that to this day is called the finest golf has ever produced.

Mickey joined the LPGA Tour in 1955, and from 1957 to 1965 there was no one who could touch her. In that time she won sixty-five tournaments, nearly a third of those she entered. Her banner year was 1961, when she won ten events including the U.S. Open, the LPGA

Above: Betsy Rawls won the U.S. Open in her rookie year and took ten titles in 1959.

Opposite: When Louise Suggs won the 1949 U.S. Open she beat Babe Zaharias by fourteen strokes.

Championship, and her own Mickey Wright Open in her hometown of San Diego.

She followed with ten more wins in 1962, a record thirteen wins in 1963, and eleven in 1964. Thereafter she went into semi-retirement to recover from nagging injuries, manage her investments, and pursue a college degree. Although Wright played sporadically during the next few years and continued to win, she had made her decision. "All I ever wanted to be was the greatest woman golfer in the world," she said, "and I quit when I believed I had done that." No one would argue. With eighty-four career victories, she is second on the LPGA's all-time list. Among her records, she twice won four consecutive events; topped the money list from 1961 through 1964; won at least one tournament a year for fourteen seasons (1956–69); and won the Vare Trophy five straight years (1960–64).

The rise of Mickey Wright mirrored the steady growth of the LPGA, which, in turn, reflected the good times in America. After two decades of depression and war, the country had emerged into a period of expansion and prosperity. For more Americans than ever before, it was time to play golf.

New courses were popping up everywhere, and they weren't quite like the old ones. It had been a quarter-century since the heyday of golf architects Tillinghast, Ross, and Mackenzie, and in that time much had happened. Earth-moving equipment had replaced horse-drawn scrapers, allowing designers to sculpt their visions from the dirt. Riding mowers had made courses easier and less expensive to maintain, while also producing mammoth greens and tees that gave the tractors room to turn around. As expanded commercial air travel brought vacation areas within easy reach, dozens of resort courses opened across America's southern tier, a region that also was helped by the development of resilient, warm-weather grasses.

The prominent architects of the twenties and thirties had all passed away, but one man stepped confidently into the breach: Robert Trent Jones. Although a fine amateur player, this Jones was no Bobby, so he turned his mind to design, becoming the first man to train specifically as a golf course architect. At Cornell University he devised his own curriculum, combining landscape design and agronomy with hydraulics, surveying, and economics. After graduation in 1930, he partnered with

Below: Robert Trent Jones was the first man to train specifically as a golf course architect.

Opposite: Mickey Wright set a new standard of excellence for women's golf.

Stanley Thompson, the leading golf architect of Canada, and by 1945 he'd solidified his reputation by collaborating with the legendary Bobby Jones on the inventive design of Atlanta's Peachtree Golf Club.

The tees at Peachtree were landing-strip length, allowing the course to be played at anywhere from six thousand to seventy-four hundred yards. The fairways were broad, but water and sand lurked at every turn. And the greens were immense, but contoured like clenched fists. Some putts were easy; others were impossible.

Peachtree was a smash hit, and it launched Trent Jones on a path of unmatched success and longevity. Today, more than five hundred courses worldwide bear the signature of Robert Trent Jones, including Spyglass Hill in California, Mauna Kea in Hawaii, and The Dunes in Myrtle Beach, as well as Dorado Beach in Puerto Rico, Sotogrande in Spain, and Royal Dar es Salaam, which Jones designed for the diversion of his friend King Hassan of Morocco.

But Trent Jones gained equal renown for his redesigns. When the USGA hired him to toughen up Oakland Hills for the 1951 Open, he produced the hardest course the pros had ever seen. It was dubbed "The Monster." Ben Hogan was the only player to better par for four rounds, and he had to play his heart out to do it. In the clubhouse, moments after his victory, Hogan encountered Jones's wife, who congratulated him on his win. "Mrs. Jones," Hogan said grimly, "if your husband had to play golf on the courses he designs, your family would be on the bread line."

Hogan won only one more Open, but Jones revamped several more Open sites, including Baltusrol, Olympic, Congressional, and Southern Hills. A classic story involves his work on the fourth hole at Baltusrol prior to the 1954 Open. Jones had transformed a rather characterless par three into an all-or-nothing shot over a broad pond, and one of the club members had deemed the new hole too difficult. Shortly after completing his work, Jones played the hole with the critic along with the club professional and the chairman of the Open. After the other three had hit their tee shots onto the green, Jones stepped up and struck a 5-iron into the cup for an ace.

"Gentlemen," he said, "I think the hole is eminently fair."

By the time that Open arrived at Baltusrol in 1954, a new era had dawned—the age of television. The fellow who launched it was a

Below: The Blue Course at Congressional Country Club, a Trent Jones design.

Opposite: The first green at Jones's Spyglass Hill Golf Club.

Overleaf: The first green at Oakland Hills, Jones's first major redesign of a U.S. Open course.

flamboyant Chicago businessman named George S. May. The P.T. Barnum of golf, May had an instinct for pleasing the public. As a young man, he traveled the revival-tent circuit hawking Bibles. It was a short step from there to becoming an efficiency expert, teaching big corporations how to work better and smarter. He earned millions, and in 1936 he bought the Tam O'Shanter Golf Club outside Chicago, reworking it so that by the mid-fifties it featured thirteen bars and a telephone on every tee.

Not surprisingly, May decided to sponsor a professional golf tournament. In 1941, he inaugurated the Tam O'Shanter Open, which would have a purse of eleven thousand dollars, the biggest in pro golf at that time. The forty-one thousand spectators were treated to a series of May's innovations. He was the first to put up grandstands so more people could follow the action; he was the first to put up scoreboards to display up-to-the-minute scores of the leading players; and, for a time, he actually pinned numbers on the backs of the players so they could be more readily identified by the gallery. He even sent one player out in a mask, billing him as "The Masked Marvel," while another, a native of Scotland, was paid to play in a kilt.

But most of all, May was the first to put golf on TV, and what a moment he chose. In 1953, for the final round of his tournament, renamed the World Championship of Golf, May positioned a single television camera atop the grandstand at the eighteenth green.

Coming to that final hole, Lew Worsham needed a birdie three to reach a playoff with Chandler Harper for the twenty-five thousand dollar first prize, once again the biggest payoff in golf at the time. After a perfect tee shot, Worsham faced a wedge approach of roughly 120 yards. His low, driving shot hit well short of the pin, but it rolled—for nearly sixty feet—and dropped straight into the hole for an eagle two and outright victory.

With that magic moment, witnessed by hundreds of thousands of incredulous viewers, everything changed as television cast its electronic glow across the fairways of professional golf. In 1954 the Open came to the tube; in 1955 The Masters; and by the early sixties every significant tournament was either on TV or trying to get there.

Below: Impresario George S. May congratulates his ace, Lew Worsham.

Opposite: The par-three fourth at Baltusrol Golf Club.

CHAPTER 9

A New Star for a New Age

With the stage set and the cameras in place, golf was ready for its first Technicolor star, Arnold Daniel Palmer. He was the classic American hero with a swaggering gait, a ready smile, and the shoulders of an NFL fullback, straight out of the hills of Western Pennsylvania. His father, Deacon, a steelworker turned golf professional, had been his only teacher, schooling him sternly in the fundamentals of good golf and good behavior.

Arnold was three years old when he first picked up a club. At age seven, he broke 100, at fourteen he shot 71 in his first high-school match, and by the time he

entered Wake Forest University he had won just about every school, county, and statewide event worth winning.

The Palmer method was less than elegant. He took a wide stance, brought the club back with a quick wrench, then lunged through impact to a club-flailing finish in which he looked as if he was snatching something out of a fire—but he powdered the ball. His putting stroke was equally ungraceful, a hunch-shouldered, knock-kneed, pigeon-toed rap. But he rapped it home from everywhere.

Above all, however, what Arnold Palmer brought to the game was a burning will to win. He had the perfect psyche for golf: a fighting spirit without a temper. Arnie gave it everything and tried everything, with a go-for-broke style that sometimes put him in trouble and a hard-nosed resourcefulness that usually got him out. He didn't play a golf course, he beat it into submission, slashing and bashing and thrashing until it had no choice but to yield.

A victory in the 1954 U.S. Amateur convinced him to turn pro, and he broke through four years later, winning the first of four Masters titles along with four other events. But it was in 1960 that Arnold Palmer truly began his reign. That April he arrived at Augusta with four wins already in his pocket, including three in succession. A first-round 67 gave him the Masters lead, and he held onto it until the final moments on Sunday when a fast-closing Ken Venturi pulled in front of him.

Palmer came to the last two holes needing two birdies to win, and in spectacular style he got them both, holing a thirty-five-footer at 17 and then knocking a 6-iron five feet from the flag at the final green. On that afternoon, the "Palmer Charge" was born.

Six weeks later it became legendary. When Arnie went to the Cherry Hills Country Club in Denver, Colorado, he had one thing in mind: a U.S. Open to go with his Masters. By the start of the final round, however, he was seven strokes off the lead, with fourteen formidable players in front of him.

In the clubhouse, shortly before heading out to play, he was approached by two friends from the press, Bob Drum and Dan Jenkins, who roasted him for his mediocre showing.

Chapter opener: Coast Guardsman Arnold Palmer with the many trophies won in amateur competition during his three-year hitch.

Opposite: A victory in the 1954 U.S. Amateur convinced Palmer to turn pro.

Below: He won sixty U.S. events and twenty-nine more around the world, along with countless fans.

"There are some guys out there who think you're just an upstart, a flash in the pan," said Drum, a Pittsburgh newspaperman who had followed Palmer for years.

"What would happen if I shot 65 in the last round?" asked Palmer testily.

"Nothing," said Drum, "you're out of it."

"It would give me a total of 280," said Palmer. "That's the kind of number that wins the U.S. Open."

"Yeah," laughed Jenkins, a Texan, "when Hogan shoots it."

More determined than ever, Palmer climbed onto the tee of the par-four first hole and did something he had tried boldly but unsuccessfully to do all week: He drove the green, 346 yards away. His two-putt birdie ignited the most explosive stretch of sub-par golf the Open had ever seen — four birdies in a row, six in the first seven holes — for a score of 30 on the outward nine.

Suddenly, Arnie was tied for the lead. Still in his path, however, was the best player of the era just past — Ben Hogan — playing side by side with the best player of the era to come —Jack Nicklaus. Hogan, at age forty-seven, was making his last serious bid at an Open title while Nicklaus, age twenty, was making his first.

But on that day in June 1960 it was Arnie's turn. He closed with a seven-under-par 65 — precisely the score he had predicted — for a two-stroke victory. When, on the eighteenth green, he leaned back and hurled his visor to the sky, Arnold Palmer was the undisputed king of American golf.

He was a king with a common man's touch. When Arnie stood on a tee, he could make eye contact with every soul in the gallery and make each of them feel he was their best friend. When he hitched up his pants, they all knew the game was on. In contrast to his stolid predecessor Hogan, Arnie wore his emotions on his sleeve. When happy, he grinned, when unhappy he grimaced, and his fans — nicknamed "Arnie's Army" — celebrated and suffered with him every step of the way.

They celebrated four Masters jackets and they suffered three playoff losses in the U.S. Open. They celebrated back-to-back victories in the British Open, a championship he single-handedly resurrected to prominence from its post-War doldrums simply by playing in it each year. And they suffered as he struggled in vain to

Left: Arnie wore his emotions on his sleeve, and his fans suffered and celebrated with him every step of the way.

win the PGA, the major title that eluded him just as the Open had eluded Sam Snead.

In all, Arnold Palmer won sixty U.S. events, plus another twenty-nine titles around the world. He led the money list four times, was the first player to win one hundred thousand dollars in a single season, and the first to reach a million dollars in career earnings. (The PGA Tour's annual award for the leading money winner is called—what else?—the Arnold Palmer Award.) And with the help of his business manager, Mark McCormack, he built those earnings into an empire worth many millions more.

But Arnie never lost his humility, or forgot the workingman's values his father had taught him. And while winning all those titles and all that money, he also won the unmatched adoration of golf fans around the world. No player, before or since, has been loved so much by so many.

Palmer's fame was aided, unintentionally, by the nearly faceless group of pros he followed. Subtract the names Ben Hogan and Sam Snead from the list of major-championship winners in the fifties and the list is, well, dull. The victors in golf's greatest tournaments included Julius Boros, Walter Burkemo, Jim Turnesa, Lionel Hebert, Dow Finsterwald, Cary Middlecoff, Art Wall, Doug Ford, Ed Furgol, and Jack Fleck. (Not to be left out is Australian Peter Thomson, who won five British Opens between 1954 and 1965, but played only occasionally in the U.S.) All were fine players, all earned their victories, some in tremendous fashion. But none excited the fans' passion the way Arnie did.

Somewhere near the top of this list was one William Earl Casper, Jr. Billy Casper, in his own quiet way, was one of the greatest golfers of all time. But he had the misfortune to follow Hogan, Snead, and Nelson, while battling Palmer and the up-and-coming Nicklaus. The public found him too conservative to be exciting, even though he subsisted for a while on a diet of buffalo, bear, rabbit, hippopotamus, and other exotic meats as a way of dealing with rare allergies. Without the fans in his corner, he was content to draw strength from his family and religion (he was a devout Mormon), and kept on winning whether anyone noticed or not.

Casper won the 1970 Masters and two U.S. Opens. The second of these Opens, in 1966 at Olympic, was his greatest moment. He beat Palmer, who was playing to break Hogan's tournament record. Casper

Below: Billy Casper toiled in the shadow of others, but was quietly one of the best players of his era.

Opposite: In the 1966 U.S. Open he came from seven strokes behind to tie Arnold Palmer whom he beat in a playoff the next day.

Above: In all, Casper won fifty-one events, including two Opens and a Masters, plus five Vardon trophies for lowest scoring average.

came from seven behind with nine holes to play, forced a playoff, then bested Arnold by four. All told, Casper walked away with fifty-one victories on the PGA Tour, and won the Vardon Trophy for low scoring average five times. Much of his success can be attributed to an unusually wristy putting stroke, effective enough that he needed only 114 (1959) and 117 (1966) putts in his Open wins. In any other time, and especially at any time other than the go-go sixties, Billy Casper could have been a superstar. Instead, he was one of the guys who occasionally got in Arnold's way.

In a sense, Arnold Palmer sold golf to the American public, and his number-one customer was another national hero, Dwight Eisenhower, who picked up the game and brought it to the White House lawn. No one loved golf more than Ike, no one played it better than Arnie, and together they spread the gospel to millions of leisure-minded Americans.

Between 1960 and 1970, golf in the United States boomed as never before. As the number of players doubled, from five to ten million, the number of courses exploded from sixty-three hundred to ten thousand: in effect, a new golf course for every day of the year for ten straight years.

However, not everyone was able to walk onto these new courses, plunk down a few dollars, and tee up. Not everyone was cheering the growing purses and young, exciting stars. Not everyone was swept up in the golf boom that saw the game grow faster than at any time since the gutta-percha ball replaced the feathery and dramatically cut the cost of playing. Golf in America was still, for many, a closed shop.

In the early sixties, freedom fighters were marching for the civil rights of a substantial segment of society, the African-Americans. The door to golf was only barely ajar to blacks, and the game was doing all it could to remain as white as it was green.

Blacks had been around golf for a long time, and not merely as caddies. As noted above, Dr. George Grant invented the wooden tee in 1899. Three years earlier, a number of professionals, most of them just a few years off the boats from Scotland, had threatened to withdraw from the second U.S. Open because John Shippen, a black, and Oscar Bunn, a Native American, were in the field at Shinnecock Hills. Theodore F. Havemeyer, president of the USGA, declared, "We are going to play this thing today even if Shippen and Bunn are the only people in it." The Open was held, and Shippen, who tied for the lead after the first round, finished fifth and won ten dollars. He eventually became a head pro, working at a number of clubs, and continued to play in the Open, finishing fifth again in 1902.

However, throughout the first half of the twentieth century, golf's officials failed to echo Havemeyer's open-mindedness. The original charter of the PGA of America, adopted in 1916, had a "Caucasian-only" clause that remained in effect until 1961. Blacks were barred from courses throughout the country, which didn't stop players like Chicago's Walter Speedy from suing for admission to public tournaments (he lost), and men like Robert Hawkins of Massachusetts from bucking the establishment and opening black-owned country clubs in the twenties. (Four black-owned clubs survive today, down from a high of twenty-seven.) In 1928, the United Golf Association was formed, giving black golfers a chance to play for small purses—usually their own entry fees—primarily on public courses that already welcomed them. Other black golf organizations formed over the years, giving talented but otherwise disenfranchised players a chance to compete and hone their games.

Above: John Shippen was the first African-American to play in a U.S. Open.

Many great golfers, like Ted Rhodes (who was the personal pro to boxer Joe Louis), Charlie Sifford, and Pete Brown, had to overcome tremendous odds and great personal indignities to play in the few events that would have them. In 1939, the USGA refused to let four black golfers qualify for the U.S. Open; nine years later, Rhodes qualified for the Open at Riviera, where he started well but eventually fell to the pressure and scrutiny and finished twenty-six strokes behind Ben Hogan.

In 1959, William Wright became the first black to win a USGA event, capturing the National Public Links Championship, and in 1964, three years after the PGA erased the Caucasians-only clause, Brown won the Waco Open, a PGA-sponsored event. Sifford, the first black to play on the pro tour, won the 1967 Greater Hartford Open (firing a final-round 64 to hold off the field) and the 1969 Los Angeles Open, but when he played in the 1969 Greater Greensboro Open, his first tournament in the South, he was heckled and subjected to racial epithets. "I don't want to repeat the things that were said to me and about me, or rehash the threats," he told an interviewer a few years ago. "But...I can tell you I didn't play too well because of the other things I had to deal with."

Most of the battles were fought quietly and behind the scenes. White America didn't hear much about the black quest for equality in golf until 1975, when Lee Elder became the first black to qualify for The Masters by winning the Monsanto Open the year before in a playoff. He missed the cut, but played in the deep South without incident. It took nearly another two decades, but in 1990, Augusta National accepted its first black member.

Although the battle for civil rights was "won" in the sixties, vestiges of the old order remained. In 1990, the PGA Championship was scheduled to be played at Shoal Creek in Birmingham, Alabama. Two months before the tournament, owner Hall Thompson was quoted in a local newspaper as saying that his club didn't discriminate, "except for blacks." Suddenly, the fourth major was in trouble. The tournament was held, but big corporations pulled their sponsorship of the tournament broadcast, and golf's ruling bodies had to confront the ugly truth of racism. The USGA and the PGA Tour ruled that clubs practicing any form of discrimination would not be allowed to hold their events; most complied, admitting black members and, in some

Above: In 1964 Pete Brown (top) became the first black player to win a PGA Tour–sponsored event. Lee Elder (below) was the first to qualify for The Masters.

Opposite: Charlie Sifford broke the color barrier as a regular on the pro tour.

cases, women, but a few chose to forego the exposure and income that came with hosting a professional tournament, preferring to retain their status quo.

In the last few years, only a few blacks have made it into the professional ranks. Among the men, Jim Thorpe, Jim Dent, and Calvin Peete were the most prominent. Althea Gibson, the tennis star, switched sports and integrated the LPGA in 1963; she was followed in the seventies by Renee Powell, whose father owns one of the few black clubs in the country. For many reasons — the disappearance of caddie programs, cost, access — there are, with the notable exception of Tiger Woods, precious few blacks on the horizon as the twenty-first century begins.

In the early sixties, as black golfers began cracking the color barrier, the rest of golf was booming, and no aspect changed more dramatically than the professional tour. For years it had been relatively stagnant. Except for the major championships and a couple of California pro-ams hosted by avid golfers Bing Crosby and Bob Hope, the tour had been a succession of modest, community-run events with names like the Rubber City Open, Nashville Invitational, and Palm Beach Round-Robin. But as the TV networks and commercial sponsors began to pay serious money for the right to beam Arnie & Co. into the homes of golf fans, pro golf became big business.

This growth did not come without pain. For a brief time, a conflict brewed among the PGA of America, the tournament sponsors, and the players over who should receive the lion's share of the broadcast fees. The result was that the players split from their teaching-pro brethren in the PGA, taking most of the rights money with them. Joseph C. Dey, the highly respected executive director of the USGA, took over as the first Commissioner of the organization that became known as the PGA Tour.

In 1958, the total purse for the tour had been one million dollars. A decade later, when the PGA Tour was formed, the purses increased to five million. For the pros, the era of big money had begun. Not suprisingly, that era produced a legion of talented young players. But one fellow rose above them all — indeed, above every professional ever to play the game: Jack Nicklaus.

Above: Calvin Peete won 11 events during a five-year span in the 1980s.

Opposite: Renee Powell played regularly on the LPGA Tour in the 1970s. Her father owns one of the few black golf clubs in the country, and she is active in the development of inner city junior golfers.

CHAPTER 10

The Player of the Century

When he came to golf at the age of ten, the chunky kid from Columbus, Ohio, had a lot on his side. In Charlie Nicklaus he had a devoted father who loved the game; in Scioto Country Club he had a home course so formidable that it had hosted a U.S. Open won by Bobby Jones; and, in Scioto's club professional, Jack Grout, he had one of the finest instructors in the country, a mentor who would drum into him the importance of a rock-steady head, good balance, and a big, powerful swing.

But most of all, Jack Nicklaus had raw athletic talent. He shot 51 for the first nine holes he played. By the

age of thirteen he had broken 70 at Scioto, and at sixteen he stunned a field full of club professionals and a handful of touring pros by winning the Ohio State Open title.

Yet during much of his youth, golf was just another game for Jack Nicklaus, something to do when he wasn't playing center on the Upper Arlington High School basketball team or catcher on the baseball team or quarterback on the football team. In a sense, although his other interests would change over the years, golf would remain just one priority among many for Jack Nicklaus. He would become, in the words of fellow player Chi Chi Rodriguez, a "legend in his spare time."

Jack's first step toward immortality came in the 1959 U.S. Amateur Championship, played at the Broadmoor Resort in Colorado, where he scored a dramatic eighteenth-hole victory in the final match over the defending champion, Charlie Coe. Two years later, he won both the Amateur and NCAA titles, and the year after that he joined the pro tour.

No player was more eagerly anticipated, and yet no player was more rudely greeted by both the press and the public. They called him "Fat Jack" and "Nick Louse," said he was too young, too heavy, too somber, and too slow. But the simple truth was he just wasn't Arnold Palmer.

The contrast between the two could not have been greater. Where Palmer warmed to the galleries, Nicklaus ignored them. As Arnie's face found a thousand expressions, Nicklaus maintained what one writer called a "state prison stare."

Their styles of play were equally diverse. While the dashing Palmer could turn an ordinary round into high drama, Jack had a knack for making even superb play look matter-of-fact. Granted, his drives were gargantuan, his irons majestic, and he putted with the touch of an angel, but he went about his business with the plodding monotony of a mailman.

The inevitable Palmer-Nicklaus showdown came halfway through Jack's rookie year, 1960, in the U.S. Open at Oakmont. Despite his glittering amateur credentials, Jack had yet to win in his first six months on tour. He had scored a second-place finish at Phoenix, but the winner that week had been Arnold Palmer, with a margin of victory of thirteen strokes.

Below: Nicklaus shared his early success with his father Charlie, a devoted golfer.

Opposite: At age sixteen, Jack beat a full field of pros to win the Ohio State Open title.

Oakmont, just a few miles from Pittsburgh, was smack in the heart of Palmer country, and Arnie's Army was never more staunchly behind their general, who treated them to four days of gallant golf. His 283 total put him in first place. But it also put him in a tie with young Nicklaus, who had wrapped himself in a week-long cocoon of concentration and played the best golf of his budding career.

In the eighteen-hole playoff, Jack gave the world its first look at a new standard of championship golf. Taking the lead at the first hole, he never let go. By the halfway mark, he was ahead by three strokes, and that became his margin of victory. Thus, in his seventeenth tournament as a professional, Nicklaus won and won big, and the tremors were felt throughout the world of golf. A geological shift had taken place.

Jack won twice more before the end of that year. Then in 1963 he exploded with five wins, including both The Masters and the PGA Championship. In a space of eighteen months, the twenty-three–year–old Nicklaus had become the man to beat, and he would remain exactly that for nearly a quarter-century.

Above: One of the few players to threaten Jack's dominance was Lee Trevino.

Opposite: By 1966, at age 26, he had become the youngest man to complete the Grand Slam.

His idol was Bobby Jones, and like Jones, Jack geared his career around the major championships, carefully managing his practice and play in order to peak for The Masters, U.S. Open, British Open, and PGA Championship. When he won the 1966 British Open at Muirfield, he became, at age twenty-six, the youngest man to complete the career Grand Slam. And that was just the beginning. Ultimately, Nicklaus would win a total of eighteen major championships—six Masters, five PGAs, four U.S. Opens, and three British Opens, a record that no other player has remotely approached, or is ever likely to. (Some fans add Jack's two U.S. Amateur titles to the list, giving him an even, and even more impressive, total of twenty.)

Nicklaus did not simply win, he won in convincing, commanding, and occasionally superhuman style. His victory in the 1965 Masters came by nine strokes with a then-record score of 271, a sustained display of dominance witnessed by Bobby Jones himself, who pronounced it "the greatest performance in golf history" and then paid Jack the ultimate compliment: "He plays a game with which I'm not familiar."

At one time or another Nicklaus held or shared the eighteen-hole and seventy-two–hole scoring records for each of the four major championships. Five times he won two majors in the same year, and in

1972 he came within a whisker of duplicating Ben Hogan's Triple Crown, winning The Masters and U.S. Open before finishing second to Lee Trevino in the British Open.

Trevino, with six major championships of his own, was one of a handful of world-class players during the 1970s and 1980s who threatened the reign of Jack Nicklaus. Another was Johnny Miller, the golden-haired Californian who burst to prominence with a 63 in the final round of the 1973 U.S. Open, at venerable and supposedly invulnerable Oakmont, and also went on to win two dozen events.

But it was Kansas City's Tom Watson who made the boldest mark of all, winning five British Opens, including a thrilling tussle with Nicklaus at Turnberry in 1977, when the two of them lapped the field on Saturday and Sunday, Nicklaus shooting rounds of 66-66, yet falling one short of Watson's 66-65. Watson also stared down Jack in both the 1977 and 1981 Masters and in the 1982 U.S. Open at Pebble Beach, where his dramatic pitch shot into the seventy-first hole gave him the birdie he needed for victory.

When Jack lost, he lost graciously, and he always came back, marshaling his mind and muscles more effectively, and over a longer period, than any player with the exception of Sam Snead. Nicklaus was winning major championships before Trevino, Miller, and Watson came along, and he was also winning them after they stopped.

In the process he also won over the fans—not with charisma and charm, as Arnie had, but with the enduring brilliance of his game.

But he wasn't unmindful of what was said about him along the way, and it hurt. So he turned his incredible self-discipline on himself. He lost weight, grew his hair (replacing a fifties' crew-cut with a seventies' Beatles mop), and traded in his white shirts and tan pants. And throughout the transformation, he kept on winning. If you cared at all about golf, if you had any interest in what could be accomplished at the highest

Below: Tom Watson after the chip shot at Pebble Beach that all but insured his victory over Nicklaus in the 1982 U.S. Open.

Opposite: In the British open at Turnberry in 1977, Watson edged Nicklaus after a titanic head-to-head battle.

Overleaf: Jack's last hurrah, the 1986 Masters.

reaches of sport, then you had to root for Jack Nicklaus. He turned the fans' grudging admiration into a sort of golf "tough love."

His last hurrah came in the 1986 Masters. By that time, he had transformed again, from the Golden Bear to the Olden Bear, from perennial favorite to sentimental favorite. He was forty-six years old and hadn't won a tournament in two years, hadn't won a major in six. Most of the media, many of his fellow competitors, and even some of his most loyal fans agreed that Jack's championship days were over.

And with nine holes to go in that 1986 Masters, they all seemed right. Nicklaus was five strokes off the lead. In order to win, he would not only have to play like blazes, he would have to beat some of the very best players from the generation that had succeeded his own.

And that is exactly what he did. With his son/caddie Jackie at his side, Nicklaus reached into his past and summoned nine holes of the most electrifying golf the game has ever seen, blitzing through the back nine at Augusta in 30 strokes. For two glorious hours, the vintage Nicklaus returned. With a display of inspired shotmaking, brilliant putting, and plain old guts, Jack roared past his young rivals to a one-stroke victory and a record sixth green jacket.

Nicklaus's career is so incomparable, it is fruitless to mention his name in the same breath as any other player of the last fifty years. No one has won more Masters, no one has won more U.S. Opens, no one has won more PGAs, and although others have won more British Opens, no one has finished second there as often as Nicklaus, who has an incredible seven runner-up finishes to go with his three victories. Indeed, along with his eighteen championship titles, Jack has finished second in the majors no fewer than nineteen times.

Perhaps the best way to put that achievement into proper perspective is to ask which two players of the modern era—from the time of Hogan, Nelson, and Snead to today's modern stars—when taken together, can claim eighteen major professional wins and nineteen runner-up finishes.

The answer is none.

In his heyday, Jack Nicklaus set a playing standard that was at once inspiring and discouraging. Inspiring in that he showed that golf, the unmasterable game, could at least be emphatically tamed. Discouraging in that, with his titanic drives and towering irons, he distanced himself from the millions of weekend golfers who continued to languish in middle-handicap mediocrity.

But that didn't stop America's amateurs from trying to emulate the greatest golfer of his, or perhaps any, generation. They tried to drive their legs toward the target as Jack did. They copied his slightly open stance, upright swing, and turning of the head on the backswing. But they didn't have his timing, strength, or resolve, and as a result, said Englishman John Jacobs, a leading instructor, Jack turned the U.S. into "a nation of slicers." He couldn't stop them from trying, but unlike so many professionals before him, he was careful, in his books and articles, to differentiate between what he was capable of doing and what the rest of us should aspire to. For very good reason did he title his best-selling book on technique *Golf My Way*. He was clearly saying, "This is how I do it. It might not be right for you."

But in the late 1960s, when Jack was hitting his peak, along came a product that definitely was right for the average Joe: the two-piece ball.

Spalding unveiled it under the name Top-Flite. The old rubber windings were replaced by a solid core covered with a synthetic substance called Surlyn, which made the ball difficult to cut while also enabling a harder hit and greater distance, particularly on iron shots. The two-piece was harsher-feeling than the three-piece wound ball, and tougher to spin and control, but it was also less expensive and lasted far longer.

Instantly, it became the darling of mid-to-high-handicappers, who saved some money, added some distance, and, after mishit shots, saw far fewer balls smiling back at them. Today, while wound balls remain the preference of most pros and low-handicap amateurs, the two-piece rules among golf's masses. The major manufacturers offer a dizzying variety of options—each, of course, with a claim of absolute aerodynamic supremacy.

Also during the late sixties, an engineer named Karsten Solheim, who had been instrumental in the creation of the first "rabbit ear" TV antennas as well as early jet airplanes, began making putters in his garage through a new process called investment-casting, in which molten metal was poured into a mold. Up to this time, all clubheads had been hand-forged: An ingot of metal was fired until red-hot, then pounded into shape. Investment-casting allowed designers to vary the look and specifications of irons for the first time in a hundred

Opposite: When Karsten Solheim, an aeronautical engineer, began making putters through the investment casting process, the golf club business changed forever.

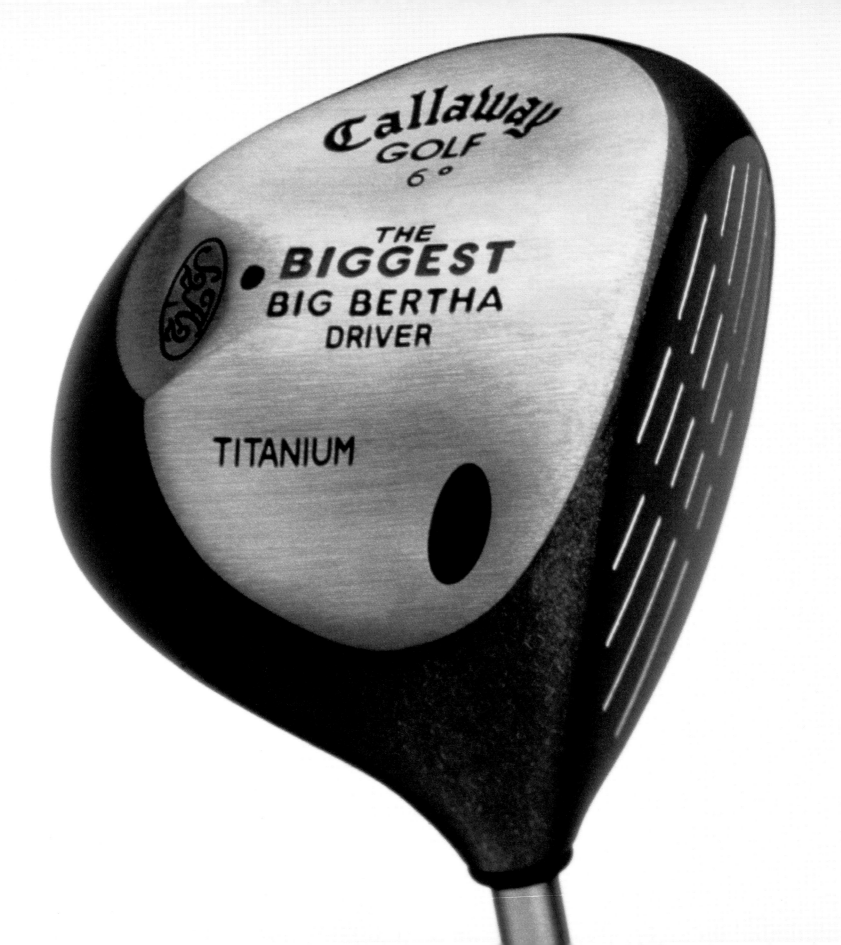

years. As a result, the mass could be moved away from the center of the club and out to its edges, creating a cavity in the back of the clubhead. This "perimeter-weighting" allowed for an expanded "sweetspot," which helped golfers compensate for shots that were hit on the toe or heel. Solheim's Ping putters and irons became the rage of the industry, and ushered in a new generation of golf equipment.

By the 1970s, investment-cast irons were common, and within a decade the same process was used to manufacture "metalwoods," which were hollow on the inside, had the weight spread to the outside, and had amateurs beside themselves over the increased distance and accuracy they'd bought.

Continued advancements in chemistry, aerodynamics, and computer-aided design have brought modern technology to the aid of golfers. Today's typical driver has a metal head the size of a grapefruit attached to a shaft made of graphite, boron, or titanium. Irons come in a range of eye-catching shapes, sizes, and even colors, and there is a utility club for every utility, from the flop wedge to the 13-wood (but, alas, the only wood in it is its name).

Meanwhile soft-spiked shoes have guaranteed smoother greens, a double-strap bag has eased the load, and for those who fight a bad back, there's even a device that tees up the ball and plucks it out of the cup.

As improvements in golf equipment began to threaten the sanctity of par, golf course architects once again rose in defense. During the 1960s, the trend started by Trent Jones toward longer and longer layouts continued, occasionally to the point of absurdity, with more than one course boasting back tees of eight thousand yards. Such monster tracks came with huge maintenance budgets that few clubs could afford.

Still, there was a general clamor for more challenging designs, fueled by the game's two leading publications, GOLF Magazine and Golf Digest, which began ranking the top courses in America and the world, with difficulty a prime criterion. Since every major developer and architect aspired to a spot on those lists, a "bigger is better" philosophy prevailed.

Then one man got a different idea. Pete Dye was an Indianapolis insurance salesman who dabbled in golf-course architecture one sum-

Below: Double-strap bags have eased the load for millions of golfers.

Opposite: The king of the modern metal woods, Callaway's Big Bertha.

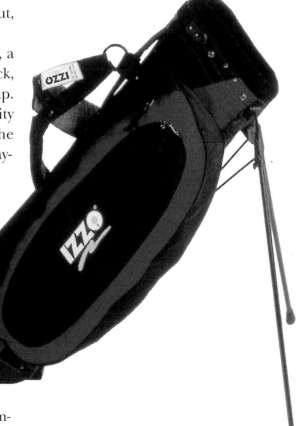

RING THE BELL
FOR MY DAD
PAUL F. DYE
WHO LOVED HIS FAMILY
AND EVERYTHING ABOUT
THE GAME OF GOLF
1956   PETE DYE

mer and never turned back. He had completed a few modest courses when, in 1963, he and wife Alice toured the great links of Scotland and were struck by their unspoiled, ageless aura. When a few years later, Dye was hired (bringing along as his assistant a rookie architect named Jack Nicklaus) to build the first course on Hilton Head Island, South Carolina, he transferred those Scottish gambits to American soil, and in so doing opened a new and exciting era of course design.

Harbour Town from the back tees was barely sixty-six hundred yards, but it was sixty-six hundred yards of architectural shrewdness, its narrow fairways winding through marshland and forests to small and fiercely defended greens. There were only thirty-five bunkers, but they were not wasted. Sand completely encircled one green whose bunker also housed a tree. Another greenside bunker was walled with cypress planks, and several greens were bulkheaded with railroad ties, an idea straight out of old Prestwick.

"It's different, but then, so was Garbo," said Dye as he unveiled his course for the 1969 Heritage Classic. Harbour Town violated just about every prevailing rule of American golf architecture and yet, by unanimous consent, it was brilliant. The ultimate stamp of approval came when that Heritage Classic was won by Arnold Palmer with a score of 283—one under par.

Harbour Town launched the career of Pete Dye, who took his artistic touch to dozens of courses across America as well as the Dominican Republic, where he created his seaside masterpiece, "The Teeth of the Dog," which is ranked among the top twenty courses in the world.

The rest of the design fraternity spent two decades emulating his work. One of his most ardent imitators was his Harbour Town collaborator, Nicklaus, who parlayed his prominence as a player into an enormously successful career as an architect. Jack's first important design came in his native Columbus, Ohio, where, in collaboration with Desmond Muirhead, he sought to do what Bobby Jones had done at Augusta—create a home course that incorporated aspects of the holes he most admired.

The Muirfield Village Golf Club was set on a tract of rolling, tree-lined land, laced with streams and ponds. It resembled

Below: Jack Nicklaus's pride and joy, the Muirfield Village Golf Club.

Opposite: Golf architecture's imaginative maverick, Pete Dye.

Augusta National in its carefully conceived contours, its elegance, and in the pristine condition of its fairways and greens, and it established Nicklaus as both a talented designer and a stickler for meticulous maintenance. That was in 1974. Today the Nicklaus portfolio is approaching two hundred courses, with designs in every corner of the world.

Jack has thus become the most prominent of a new breed, the player-architect. Through a combination of his celebrity and his cost-intensive methods, he has commanded huge fees for his work — a million dollars and more just for the blueprints. As the saying goes, "Trent Jones made golf-course architecture a business, Pete Dye made it an art, and Jack Nicklaus made it lucrative."

But the most influential figure in modern course design was neither Dye nor Nicklaus. It was Deane Beman. In the late seventies, shortly after becoming Commissioner of the PGA Tour, Beman, a former Tour player, devised a plan to expand the Tour's revenues through the construction of what he called "Stadium Courses," layouts owned and operated by the Tour and designed specifically to host professional tournaments.

The first of these was the Tournament Players Course, or TPC, at Sawgrass, the Tour's headquarters in north Florida, where Beman teamed with Pete Dye on an astonishing design. Each hole was created expressly for the viewing pleasure of the gallery. There were no blind shots, no elevated greens, no trees in the line of sight. Man-made knolls, called "spectator mounds," flanked the fairways, and the dramatic eighteenth hole played to an earthen grandstand that accommodated thirty thousand people, each with a perfect view.

At the same time, Beman and Dye produced a course that is a severe test of what is now known as "target golf." With trees, water, sand, and scrub menacing every inch of the original Stadium Course, the only way to stay out of trouble was to hop carefully from lily-pad fairways to lily-pad greens. There was no room to run the ball; only a high-flying dart could hit and hold the fast and demonically sloped greens.

The most dramatic example was the seventeenth hole,

Below: The creator of Stadium Golf, former PGA Tour Commissioner Deane Beman.

Opposite: The island green seventeenth hole at the TPC at Sawgrass, site of the annual Players Championship.

a sink-or-swim par three of 133 yards to a green surrounded by water. In the first round of the 1984 Players Championship, a strong wind came up and the best players in the world put a combined sixty-four balls into the water. The stroke average that day was 3.79, the most over par ever recorded for a hole on the PGA Tour.

Unquestionably, number seventeen made a splash, and in a short time, island greens were popping up around the world, including a floating version at the Coeur d'Alene resort in Idaho. Meanwhile, Stadium Courses similar to Sawgrass took shape in ten states and three foreign countries, and target golf became the design craze of the 1980s.

Many TPC projects paired a trained golf architect with a Tour player "advisor," launching several prominent golfers into the profitable avocation of course design. Today, more than a dozen players are active architects, with Tom Weiskopf, Jerry Pate, Mark McCumber, and Ben Crenshaw among the most successful and best respected.

But the majority of top jobs still go to Dye, to Nicklaus, and to a handful of established masters. Chief among these is Tom Fazio, highly revered for his ability to craft beautiful and natural-looking holes, which he has shown in courses ranging from Galloway National in New Jersey to Black Diamond in Florida to his most stunning achievement, Shadow Creek, a patch of North Carolina forest plopped down in the middle of Nevada desert.

At the behest of casino owner Steve Wynn, and at a record cost of thirty-seven million, Fazio transformed three hundred acres of flat and desolate terrain just a few miles from the Vegas Strip into lush, rolling meadowland, with hundreds of transplanted pine trees, a network of man-made streams, and a zoo's worth of waterfowl and birds. Utterly Las Vegas, it is the most artificial course in the world, and yet it looks perfectly natural.

Flanking Fazio at the top of the architectural world are the two sons of Robert Trent Jones. Bobby carries not only his father's name but his commitment to innovative, strategic design, with the Prince course in Hawaii and Spanish Bay in California two of his best examples. Meanwhile, brother Rees has earned widespread respect both for his own designs and for his inspired renovations of classic courses. In the footsteps of his father, Rees has become the "Open Doctor," the man the USGA calls upon to strengthen its sites for the national championship.

It was Rees Jones who also was called to Daytona Beach, Florida, in 1993 to design the first home course for the LPGA, a group of ladies who've come a long, long way.

With the retirement of Mickey Wright, a void had been left in women's golf. But, as one of her successors, Judy Rankin, observed, "Mickey got the outside world to take a second look at women's golf, and when they looked, they discovered the rest of us."

The first one they noticed was a tall Texan named Kathy Whitworth, who turned pro in 1959 and led the LPGA money list in eight of the nine years between 1965 and 1973. She also helped lead the tour from the near-obscurity of the early sixties into the bright lights of the eighties.

No player in history, man or woman, has amassed more official victories than Whitworth, who finished her career with eighty-eight wins, four more than Sam Snead. In the process, she became the first

Above: The ninth hole at the LPGA International in Daytona Beach.

Opposite: Three of the giants of golf architecture today, Tom Fazio, Robert Trent Jones III, and Rees Jones.

woman golfer to surpass one million dollars in official prize winnings at a time when purses were so small that she didn't win more than fifty thousand dollars in any year until 1972. (Her first victory, in 1962, earned her thirteen hundred; her last, in 1985, was worth thirty thousand dollars.) Along the way, she captured the LPGA Championship three times and the Vare Trophy for low scoring average six times, but (shades of Snead) never the U.S. Women's Open.

At the age of fifteen, Judy Rankin (although then her last name was Torluemke) was the leading amateur in the U.S. Women's Open. At age seventeen, in 1962, she turned professional. Her career was respectable but un-remarkable until 1969, when she began a stretch of fine play and finishes that placed her in the top ten in money on the LPGA Tour every year through 1977. Her great-est milestone came in 1976, when she became the first woman to break the hundred-thousand-dollar barrier for a single season, winning seven events. Perhaps even more incredibly, from 1968 through 1979 she never missed a cut in the tournaments she entered. However, she won only one women's major, the 1977 Peter Jackson, although she managed second-place finishes in the Open and LPGA Championship. Much like Whitworth, Rankin went about her business in a decidedly unspectacular fashion, and both were largely unappreciated in their day.

Then there was JoAnne Carner, a long-hitting, crowd-pleasing character in the tradition of Babe Zaharias. Her maiden name was Gunderson, and as an amateur she was known as "The Great Gundy." And great she was, winning every major title in sight, including the U.S. Women's Amateur five times and playing on four consecutive Curtis Cup teams. In 1969, she became the last amateur to win an LPGA Tour event; the next year, at age thirty, she turned pro and lost little time making her mark. In the decade-and-a-half beginning in 1970 she won forty-two LPGA titles — including two Women's Opens — plus five Vardon Trophies, three Player of the Year awards, and more than three million dollars in prize money. As her tour nickname suggested, "Big Momma" added a major dash of color to women's golf.

Above: With eighty-eight victories, Kathy Whitworth is the winningest golfer of all time.

Opposite: In 1976 Judy Rankin became the first woman to surpass $100,000 in single-season earnings.

Above: JoAnne Carner followed a glittering amateur career with an equally glittering professional career.

Opposite: The LPGA's marquee player for nearly a quarter century has been Nancy Lopez.

In 1975, a young New York marketing mogul named Ray Volpe took over as Commissioner of the LPGA. He stayed only seven years, but under his aggressive and imaginative leadership the tour's purses quadrupled while the televised events jumped from two to fourteen. During the same time, women's golf teams sprung up in colleges and universities across the county in response to the Title IX legislation that mandated equal funding for athletic programs for women and men.

The net effect of all this was that more and more talented women began joining the LPGA Tour. One of them was named Nancy Lopez, and in this smiling young lady from Roswell, New Mexico, the LPGA found its first certified superstar.

Like Arnold Palmer on the men's side, Lopez arrived just in time for television and oh, did she put on a show. Her rookie year, 1978, was nothing short of phenomenal. She scored back-to-back victories before the season was two months old, and then, beginning in May, she won the next five events she entered — including the LPGA Championship — while capturing the attention and affection of sports fans everywhere. Before the year was out, Lopez had won nine times, established a new season scoring average, and earned more prize money than any rookie golfer, man or woman.

From there she just got better and better, winning fifty tournaments along with legions of fans. Lopez remained the LPGA Tour's marquee attraction for twenty years.

At the same time, the supporting cast became stronger, deeper, and more compelling than ever as players such as Pat Bradley, Beth Daniel, Amy Alcott, Patty Sheehan, and Betsy King took turns at the top and brought women's professional golf to a new level of prominence. "The best women golfers in the world" is how the LPGA began billing itself, and today that is literally true, as Sweden's Annika Sorenstam, Australia's Karrie Webb, England's Laura Davies, and South Korea's Se Ri Pak are the dominant players on a tour that has expanded its reach to include events in Canada, England, Australia, Japan, and

South Korea while providing the world's best competition for players from all those countries and more.

But if there was a success story in golf — or in all of sport — during the last quarter of the twentieth century, it was unquestionably the emergence of the PGA Senior Tour.

It started in 1978 with a made-for-television event called the Legends of Golf, which brought together two-man teams of seniors in a better-ball competition at the Onion Creek Club in Austin, Texas. With NBC telecasting the Sunday afternoon finish, sixty-six–year–old Sam Snead birdied the last two holes to put him and partner Gardner Dickinson in a playoff with the Australian duo of Peter Thomson and Kel Nagle. Snead birdied the first playoff hole to cap a finale worthy of Hollywood.

The television ratings were suprisingly high, and in year two they went through the roof as the oldsters staged a show that not even Frank Capra would have dared to script. In a sudden-death playoff, Julius Boros and Roberto de Vicenzo, who'd won majors in the 1950s and 1960s, strung together an incredible six straight birdies to edge the team of Tommy Bolt and Art Wall, who had matched them birdie-for-birdie for the first five holes. Suddenly, the world realized that these guys could still play!

Flush with their success, a group of senior players, led by Boros and Snead, set up a meeting with PGA Tour Commissioner Beman to explore the notion of a tour for the over-fifty set. The next year, two modest events were held, and from that beginning the Senior PGA Tour has mushroomed into a forty-two–event tour with total prize money of forty-five million. In 1997, the Senior Tour's leading money winner, Hale Irwin, took home $2.3 million, more than any player on the regular PGA Tour; he held onto that record, and won even more money, in 1998.

The seniors succeeded because they worked at it. They knew that corporate advertising support was the most important ingredient, so they charmed their CEO patrons and cajoled their pro-am partners, sharing not only rounds of golf but rounds of drinks and stories at the nineteenth hole. The old boys were just happy to be out there, and it showed.

For guys like Mike Hill, the Senior Tour was a godsend. He'd had

a mediocre career on the "junior" tour, winning three events and nearly six hundred thousand dollars in the seventies. In 1989, he was running a nine-hole course in Michigan and had sixteen thousand dollars to his name. By 1991, he had won more than two million dollars. For others, like Lee Trevino and Ray Floyd, the Senior Tour was the opportunity to extend their winning careers and stave off retirement. And for Arnold Palmer, it was the ideal way to sustain the encouragement and affection of his fans. Yes, the Senior Tour was the ultimate second chance, the greatest mulligan in golf.

Above: Hale Irwin (left) has dominated the Senior Tour as no man before him, while Arnold Palmer continues to be the favorite of the galleries.

CHAPTER 11

The Game
for All

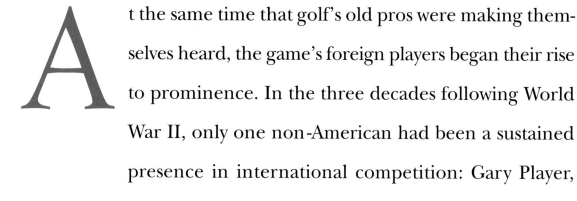

A t the same time that golf's old pros were making themselves heard, the game's foreign players began their rise to prominence. In the three decades following World War II, only one non-American had been a sustained presence in international competition: Gary Player, the emphatic little South African who in the 1960s stood alongside Nicklaus and Palmer as one of golf's "big three."

Well before commercial air travel became commonplace, the peripatetic Player was buzzing around the globe. No athlete has logged more miles, and no golfer has won more events worldwide, 185 at last count.

Nine of those wins are major championships, and when he won the 1965 U.S. Open at Hazeltine, Player joined Hogan and Sarazen in an elite club, that would soon include Nicklaus, as the only players to complete a modern Grand Slam of victories in the four major championships.

Player's is a most unlikely story. He was small and slight, but devoted himself to a regimen of physical training in an era where the heaviest thing the pros lifted after a round was a drink. He began with a strong grip and flat swing, but when he brought them to Europe in the late 1950s, he was laughed at; the best he could hope for, he was told, was a club job back home in South Africa. But displaying a work ethic worthy of another small man, Ben Hogan, Player transformed his play, concentrating on the short game (particularly sand play and putting), and became a consistent winner in every corner of the globe. He also gave himself over to special diets and an all-black wardrobe, and channeled his intensity into becoming the best player he could be.

Occasionally he would touch down in America, where, even with his limited schedule, he won a U.S. Open, two PGA Championships, and three Masters. (In the process, he became the first foreigner to win the PGA and The Masters, and the first since 1920 to win the Open.) And he continued to play in Europe, where he won three British Opens. The most dramatic of Player's major victories was his last, the 1978 Masters, where he birdied seven of his final ten holes for a 64 that took the title by one stroke.

The exuberant young man who hugged Gary Player on Augusta National's seventy-second green that day in 1978 would become his successor on the world stage: Severiano Ballesteros. Born in the village of Pedrena, on the northern coast of Spain, Seve was the youngest of four brothers, all of them golf professionals. Beginning at age six, he taught himself the game, practicing endlessly on the beach with just one club, an old cut-down 3-iron that he learned to hit a dozen different ways. By the time he was carrying a full set, Seve had a talent for recovery and inventive shotmaking that was utterly without peer. He was playing off scratch at age thirteen, and turned pro at sixteen.

At age nineteen, he stunned the world by taking the fifty-four–hole lead in the British Open at Royal Birkdale. He slipped back into a tie for second behind Johnny Miller, but three years later, in 1979, he took

Opposite: The most charismatic player Europe has ever produced, Seve Ballesteros of Spain.

Chapter opener: Gary Player gets the green jacket from Tom Watson at the 1978 Masters.

the title at Royal Lytham when he beat Jack Nicklaus by three strokes. His play on the sixteenth hole the final day was a perfect example of Ballesteros magic: He hit his tee shot into the car park adjacent to the hole, from where he pitched to fifteen feet and holed the birdie putt. He also won another European tour event that year, as well as that tour's money title and Vardon Trophy for low scoring average. The following spring he scored a wire-to-wire victory in The Masters and thereby established himself as the best young player—and the best non-American player—in the world.

Before he was done, Ballesteros would win two Masters, three British Opens, and the national titles of nine different countries. He also compiled an outstanding record as a member of eight Ryder Cup teams, where his short-game skills and imagination made him a star both in the singles and two-man play.

Seve's success on the world stage, especially in the Ryder Cup, inspired his colleagues on the European circuit and set in motion a shift in golf's international balance of power. Ballesteros was followed in Augusta's winner's circle by his talented countryman Jose Maria Olazabal (Seve's regular partner in Ryder Cup foursomes and four-balls), as well as Scotland's Sandy Lyle (who also won a British Open), Ian Woosnam of Wales, Bernhard Langer of Germany (with two green jackets) and England's Nick Faldo (with three). Indeed, between 1985 and 1996, eight of the twelve Masters titles went to European players.

Meanwhile, in the eleven years from 1984 through 1994, only one American finished first in the British Open as Faldo led the way with three victories to match his trio of Masters wins.

Clearly, the tide had turned. But the most telling evidence came in the Ryder Cup, where Great Britain had been America's whipping boy for half a century, with only three wins in twenty-three encounters. The agent of change was Jack Nicklaus, who suggested to the Brits that they expand their side to include European players. Once they did, beginning in 1979, everything changed. In the ten matches since 1979, America has won five times and Europe four, with one tie (meaning that Europe, the defending champion, kept the cup). With virtually every contest a cliffhanger, the Ryder Cup has become golf's most electrifying event. In the most recent staging, at Valderrama in Spain, the outcome came down to the final green of the last match on the course,

Below: Colin Montgomerie sinks the Ryder Cup winning putt at Valderrama, 1997.

Over the last decade or so, most of the Masters green jackets have gone across the Atlantic. England's Nick Faldo (left) owns three and Bernhard Langer (above) of Germany two.

when Europe's leading player, Colin Montgomerie of Scotland, clinched the win. Appropriately, the lion's share of the credit for that victory went to the team captain, Seve Ballesteros.

But by no means has the awakening of golf's international talent been confined to Europe. Zimbabwe's Nick Price has won a British Open and two PGA Championships along with three dozen events in the U.S. and around the globe, while the precocious South African Ernie Els has won two of the last five U.S. Opens and, at age twenty-seven, ranks among the top five players in the world.

And for most of the last ten years, the world's number-one golfer has been an extraordinarily gifted player from Queensland, Australia: the Great White Shark, Greg Norman.

Norman was twenty-eight when he came full-time to America in 1983 with two dozen international titles already in his pocket. Over the next decade and a half, he added another fifty victories in the U.S. and abroad, far more than any other player.

Norman's most productive year was 1986, when he had seven wins, including the British Open and a string of six straight events across the European and Australian tours. But as good as that season was, it might have been much better. For 1986 was the year of Norman's "Saturday Slam," when he held the lead in each of the four major championships with one round to go, but came up empty in The Masters, U.S. Open, and PGA Championship.

Indeed, for all his success, Greg Norman is perhaps best known for his frustration and failure in the major championships. In the 1986 PGA, a bunker shot on the last hole — and into the last hole — by Bob Tway stole the title; in the 1997 Masters underdog Larry Mize played the shot of his life on the second hole of sudden-death, chipping in from more than one hundred feet away; and in the 1996 Masters Norman simply beat himself, squandering a six-stroke lead with an inglorious 78 that opened the door for Nick Faldo. Norman has only two major championships — the 1986 and 1993 British Opens — and has

Above: Zimbabwe's Nick Price has won a PGA, two British Opens, and three dozen events around the world.

Opposite, clockwise: Three more Masters Champions, Scotsman Sandy Lyle (upper left), Welshman Ian Woosnam, and Spain's Jose Maria Olazabal.

finished second in the majors an agonizing eight times, including a playoff loss in each of the four events.

Still, with his broad shoulders, white-blonde hair, and blinding smile, Greg Norman has become a worldwide icon, golf's phenomenon of the global-marketing age. When he came to America in the early eighties, the pros were playing for a total purse of seventeen million a year. Today, the PGA Tour is an international circuit—a mini-World Tour—playing for more than one hundred million, and Norman has been both a catalyst and a beneficiary of that explosion.

The first player to surpass ten million dollars in earnings on the course, he has made at least ten times that off it in business ventures that range from yacht building to men's apparel to turfgrass cultivation, and his familiar face and figure appear on buses and billboards from Tokyo to Times Square.

These days, every aspect of golf is more visible than ever. Not a weekend goes by when the game isn't beamed into our living rooms, whether from the men's tour, the LPGA, the Seniors, or some form of made-for-TV golf—only half-jokingly referred to as the "Silly Season"—from the

Above: Bob Tway holes out at 18 to win the 1986 PGA.

Opposite: The man who was beaten so dramatically by Tway—and others during his career—Greg Norman, en route to victory in the 1986 British Open at Turnberry.

Above: Club-making mogul Ely Callaway on a bed of Big Berthas.

Opposite: The man who made golf cool, Tiger Woods.

Skins Game to the World Putting Championship. Golf tournaments can be found on all the major networks, many of the not-so-major ones, and even has The Golf Channel, a twenty-four-hour-a-day cable network devoted to you-know-what. There are more golf publications than ever before, and the stores are glutted with books and videos on how to play the game. The top teaching pros, like David Leadbetter, have become stars, and the top clubmakers, like Ely Callaway, have become saviors to the struggling masses, as commerce in the game continues to soar.

Yes, golf is hot, and now, for the first time, it is also cool, with the emergence of Eldrick Tiger Woods.

He was gripping a club before he could walk, and by the time he was two he was playing the game, and playing it better than any two-year-old in history. It was all part of a master plan, carefully scripted by his father Earl, a Vietnam Green Beret who believed that the next generation of great players would be those who were introduced to the game before they were a year old.

So by the time he was in the second grade, Tiger was listening to motivational tapes, carrying a one-iron, and winning tournaments for kids twice his age. He also was being schooled in competitiveness, learning to hole putts while Earl jingled the change in his pockets.

One day he came home from school and tacked a piece of paper on his bedroom. It listed golf's major championships, and next to each one Tiger recorded the age of Jack Nicklaus at the time he won each championship for the first time. These would be Tiger's goals: To do what Nicklaus did, only sooner.

But first, he entered a tournament Jack had never tried, the U.S. Junior Amateur Championship, and at age fifteen he became the youngest champion in the tournament's history. No one had ever won the Junior Amateur more than once, but Tiger won it three years in a row.

Then, in 1994 at the TPC at Sawgrass, he came from five holes down in the final match of the U.S. Amateur to win the title. He was eighteen years old—one year younger than Nicklaus in 1959 and, once again, the youngest ever to win the championship.

Right: The ultimate proof of golf's surge into the age of marketing: Tiger on a Wheaties box.

But Nicklaus had won the Amateur twice by the time he was twenty-one. So what did Tiger do? He won it three times by the age of twenty—and three times in a row, a feat that no one, not even Bobby Jones, had managed to pull off. And he won that third title in breathtaking style, once again coming from five holes down in the final match at Pumpkin Ridge in Oregon.

By the time he turned pro a few weeks later, Tiger Woods was a rich young man, with sixty million dollars worth of commercial endorsements. There is no doubt but that he gave his sponsors their money's worth, winning twice in his first seven starts, and was later named Sports Illustrated's Sportsman of the Year for 1996.

And yet, by his own reckoning, he hadn't played his best. That was saved for April of 1997, when Tiger Woods did what no player of the twentieth century had ever done to a course, a field of challengers, or a major championship. He won The Masters, his first major as a professional, by a record-breaking twelve strokes. When the green jacket was slipped on his shoulders he was twenty-one years old, two years younger than Nicklaus had been in 1963.

With his staggering distance off the tee, a fearless imagination around the green, and a mental toughness that belies his tender years, Tiger Woods sent a shock wave through professional golf, and raised the bar for the world's best players.

Perhaps more important, he captured the attention of millions of people, many of whom had never considered playing golf. Tiger's father is one-quarter Native American, one-quarter Chinese, and half African-American. His mother is one-quarter Chinese, one-quarter white, and half Thai. And so, at the same time that Tiger broke records at Augusta, he broke barriers and scored a major victory for minority golfers.

Today, for the first time, thousands of young Americans of every ethnic and racial background are turning to golf. New courses are opening at the rate of more than four hundred a year, and junior programs that once were ignored now are bursting at the seams.

The game's major associations have responded, too, with the funds and facilities needed to welcome new players. Golf, despite its considerable cost, its damnable difficulty, and its puttering pace, is once again becoming a game for the masses.

And the growth is not limited to America. In Europe, the expansion ignited by Ballesteros and his colleagues continues, with public courses sprouting all over Germany, while France closes in on a golf population of one million. In Sweden, they take the game so seriously that all new players must pass a proficiency test, but that hasn't stopped the ranks of Swedish golfers from quadrupling in the past decade, producing several of the world's best young professionals through a national program reminiscent of what the Swedes did in tennis back in the 1970s.

In the Far East, Thailand, Malaysia, and Singapore all have seen course-construction booms, and three years ago, when the first public golf course was opened in a suburb of Hong Kong, ten thousand people took up the game.

In Japan, a scarcity of land for golf courses means that only the super-rich can afford to actually play. Everyone else is relegated to the driving range. But that hasn't diminished either the enthusiasm or the numbers of Japanese golfers, now fifteen million strong. And Japan is also a leading exporter of golf equipment, especially clubs that are among the first to use the latest high-tech designs and exotic materials.

Today there are golf courses in Luxembourg and Israel, in Pakistan and Guatemala, in Barbados and Iceland — even in Russia and China. (Both countries have national training institutes designed to produce not only world-class players but teachers who can spread the gospel at home.) The game is played in eighty different nations, on more than twenty-five thousand courses, by close to fifty million people.

Yes, fifty million people play this game that increases the blood pressure, ruins the disposition, spoils digestion, hurts the eyes, calluses the hands, and makes liars out of honest men and fools out of everyone. Once addicted, no golfer ever turns back. The lure is eternal.

And so, as we approach a new millennium, the future of golf seems boundless. Royal and ancient and utterly irresistible, it truly is the game of a lifetime.

Above: Jesper Parnevik leads an ever-growing pack of strong young professionals from Sweden.

Opposite: No nation is more addicted to golf than Japan with 15 million players, many of whom never get past the driving range.

Overleaf: U.S. Open, 1996.

Bibliography

Alliss, Peter, *The Who's Who of Golf*, Prentice-Hall: Englewood Cliffs, N.J., 1983.

Barkow, Al, *The History of the PGA Tour*, Doubleday: New York, 1989.

Concannon, Dale, *Golf–The Early Days*, Smithmark: New York, 1995.

Cornish, Geoffrey S. and Ronald E. Whitten, *The Architects of Golf*, Harper-Collins: New York, 1981.

Editors of GOLF Magazine, *GOLF Magazine's Encyclopedia of Golf* (Second Edition), HarperCollins: New York, 1993.

Gleason, Dan, *The Great, The Grand and the Also-Ran*, Random House: New York, 1976.

Green, Robert, *An Illustrated History of Golf*, London, 1987.

Henderson, Ian T. and David I. Stirk, *Golf In The Making* (Revised Edition), Sean Arnold: London, 1994.

Holloway, Robinson, outline of African-American history in golf (private).

McCord, Robert R., *Golf–An Album of its History*, Burford Books: Short Hills, N.J., 1998.

Peper, George and the Editors of GOLF Magazine, *Golf in America: The First 100 Years*, Harry N. Abrams, Inc.: New York, 1988.

Peper, George and James A. Frank, Lorin Anderson, and John Andrisani, *GOLF Magazine's Complete Book of Golf Instruction*, Harry N. Abrams, Inc.: New York, 1997.

Price, Charles, *The World of Golf*, Random House: New York, 1962.

Quirin, Dr. Bill, *Golf Clubs of the MGA*, Golf Magazine Properties: New York, 1997.

Sampson, Curt, *Hogan*, Rutledge Hill Press: Nashville, Tenn., 1996.

Sampson, Curt, *The Masters*, Villard: New York, 1998.

Sinnette, Calvin H., *Forbidden Fairways: African Americans and the Game of Golf*, Sleeping Bear Press: Chelsea, Mich., 1998.

Stanley, Louis T., *St. Andrews–The Home of Golf*, Salem House: Topsfield, Mass., 1986.

Steel, Donald and Peter Ryde, editors, *The Encyclopedia of Golf*, Viking: New York, 1975.

Vardon, Harry, *The Complete Golfer*, Methuen: London, 1921.

Wind, Herbert Warren, *The Story of American Golf*, Simon and Schuster: New York, 1956.

Wiren, Gary, *The PGA Manual of Golf*, Macmillan: New York, 1991.

Index

(Numbers in italics refer to illustrations.)

About the Author

George Peper is the Editor-in-Chief of GOLF Magazine and Editorial Director of GOLF Magazine Properties, a publishing network that includes the Met Golfer, the AT&T Pebble Beach Pro-Am program, the PGA Tour Championship program, and, in 1995, the official magazines for the U.S. Open, Women's Open, and Senior Open Championships.

He has been chief of the editorial operation at GOLF Magazine since 1977, having joined the magazine as an Associate Editor in 1976. Under his tenure, GOLF Magazine has become the fastest-growing publication in the game, more than doubling in circulation to its current rate base of 1.4 million, while also becoming the only golf publication to earn three nominations for the prestigious National Magazine Award.

Peper has written or edited ten books on golf, including the First Edition of *Golf Courses of the PGA Tour*, a best-seller and selection (as is the current, second edition) of the Book of the Month Club. Since 1983, he has also been Editor of the *Masters Annual*, the official chronicle of the Masters Tournament, and in 1994, served as Editorial Consultant to the USGA's centennial film series, "Heroes of the Game."

Peper has a B.A. in English and Comparative Literature from Princeton University. A 6-handicap golfer, he has played most of the courses in his latest book and is a member of the Sleepy Hollow Country Club (NY), as well as four clubs in Scotland: Loch Lomond, The Carnegie Club, Turnberry, and the Royal and Ancient Golf Club of St. Andrews.

His wife, Libby, is a well-known illustrator specializing in golf courses. Her vivid oil-painted maps illustrate *Golf Courses on the PGA Tour*, and her schematic views of golf holes appear frequently in a variety of golf publications.

The Pepers live in Grandview, NY, with their sons, Tim and Scott.

Picture Credits

The pictures in this book were provided courtesy of the following:

Acme Photo: pp. 110, 128.

AP/World Wide Photos: pp. 99, 124, 132, 139, 166, 167, 168.

Callaway Golf: p. 186.

The Dale Concannon Collection at The Phil Sheldon Golf Picture Library: pp. 10, 15, 16, 43, 44 (top), 45, 47, 66, 102.

GOLF Magazine: pp. 37, 44 (bottom), 49, 52, 57, 60, 61, 62, 67, 71, 72, 76, 78 (bottom), 79, 80, 90, 96, 98, 105, 122, 126, 130, 136, 146, 147, 149, 159, 165, 169, 170, 171 (bottom), 172, 173, 176, 179, 192 (top and middle), 216–17.

General Mills: p. 212.

Sam Greenwood/GOLF Magazine: pp. 36, 193, 207.

Hobbs Golf Collection: pp. 12, 14, 17, 20, 22, 34 (bottom), 35, 38, 40, 41, 42, 68, 74, 75, 81, 97, 145, 214.

Izzo: p. 187.

Karsten Manufacturing Corp: p. 185.

Russell Kirk: p. 192 (bottom).

Mike Klemme/Golfoto: pp. 112–13.

The LPGA: p. 193.

Phil Sheldon: pp. 24, 26, 28–29, 46 (top), 174, 180, 181, 182, 195, 197, 200, 203, 208, 209.

The United States Golf Association's Archive Photo Collection: pp. 3 (inset), 8, 31, 34 (top), 39, 46 (bottom), 53, 55, 56, 58–59, 63, 64, 70, 73, 77, 78 (top), 87, 88, 91, 92, 93, 94, 100, 107, 114, 119, 131, 135, 142, 148, 153, 177.

UPI/Corbis-Bettmann: pp. 18–19, 21, 30, 32, 50, 54, 106, 108, 109, 111, 120, 123, 127, 137, 140, 144, 150, 151, 152, 162, 163, 171 (top), 178, 194.

Fred Vance: p. 196.

Fred Vuich/GOLF Magazine: pp. 2–3, 25, 27, 33, 82–83, 84–85, 86, 115, 116, 154, 155, 156–57, 158, 188, 189, 190, 191, 199, 204, 205, 206, 210, 211, 215.

Wilson Sportpix: p. 160.

"The Story of Golf" is a two-hour documentary film produced with the enthusiastic cooperation of the United States Golf Association and The Royal & Ancient Golf Club of St. Andrews, Scotland, by Cramer Productions, Inc., in association with the Carver Group, Inc., and distributed by APT Programs for Public Television with funding from Deloitte & Touche.